THE TIMES

HOW TO SUCCEED AT AN ASSESSMENT CENTRE

TEST-TAKING ADVICE FROM THE EXPERTS

HARRY TOLLEY & ROBERT WOOD

KOGAN PAGE

First published in 2001
Reprinted in 2002

Kogan Page Limited
120 Pentonville Road
London
N1 9JN

The views expressed in this book are those of the authors, and are not necessarily the same as those of Times Newspapers Ltd.

British Library Cataloguing in Publication Data

A CIP record for this book is available from the British Library.

ISBN 0 7494 3478 3

Typeset by Jean Cussons Typesetting, Diss, Norfolk
Printed and bound in Great Britain by Clays Ltd, St Ives plc

Contents

Contents

About the authors

Dr Harry Tolley is a special professor in the School of Education at the University of Nottingham, and also works as a researcher, author and freelance consultant. He is the co-author of *How to Pass Numeracy Tests*, *How to Pass Verbal Reasoning Tests* and *How to Pass the Police Initial Recruitment Test*, published by Kogan Page.

Dr Robert Wood is a special professor in the School of Education at the University of Nottingham. Up until recently he was a partner with Pearn Kandola Occupational Psychologists. He now works as an author and freelance consultant. He has written and co-written numerous books and papers based on his extensive experience in recruitment, assessment and selection.

Introduction

Until recently, many of the candidates who successfully negotiated a job or a promotion interview were rewarded with an invitation to attend for a second interview. This was often similar to the first, although the chances are that the questions would have been more searching and the candidates would have had to face a panel rather than a single interviewer. However, employers have now come to realize that such procedures are critically flawed as a means of recruiting new staff and as a method of selecting employees for promotion or further training. For example:

- selection based purely on interviews is likely to be subjective because of the importance attached to first impressions and the possibility of stereotyping and bias on the part of the interviewers;
- even with skilled and experienced interviewers, a second interview can easily cover the same issues in a similar way to the first;
- interviews do not provide organizations with enough information about the capability of candidates to meet the requirements of the job or the course of training for which they have applied.

Consequently, there are serious doubts about both the validity and reliability of interviews as the sole means of selecting staff. One recruitment specialist summed this up as follows: 'It is probably the worst way to recruit. You may as well just toss a coin' (Angela Baron, Institute of Personnel and Development, cited in an article in *Daily Telegraph Business File*, 29 April 1999).

In the interests of efficiency and cost effectiveness organizations are now seeking to select staff who have the competencies that match the precise needs of the job or the course of training. They have concluded, therefore, that the more information they have about the ability and personality of candidates the less are the chances of making the costly mistake of appointing, promoting or selecting someone who is unsuitable. Thus, more and more of the applicants for jobs, promotion and further training now face a multiple assessment approach as part of the recruitment–selection process. Such assessments will often be conducted by means of an assessment centre over an extended period of time – days (but typically no more than three) rather than hours. Note that the term 'assessment centre' refers to a process rather than a location; a term like 'extended assessment event' would do just as well.

Assessment centres involve both time and expense, so employers tend to use them after the initial stages of the selection process have enabled them to draw up a shortlist of candidates who, on the evidence available, appear to match the selection criteria. Assessment centres themselves are highly structured in terms both of their programmes and assessment activities. In some cases they will be run by human resources staff from within the organization, assisted, as appropriate, by other people such as senior managers. In other situations recruitment professionals from outside the organization, such as occupational psychologists, may be involved as consultants.

The structure and content of the programmes of assessment

centres vary according to the precise details of the job or training opportunity on offer. For example, a post in management might involve a combination of the following activities: an in-tray exercise; group problem solving; a case study; presentation; ability tests and personality inventories/questionnaires. For jobs in other types of employment there may well be a greater emphasis on, for example, creativity or information technology (IT) and written communication skills.

Whatever the activities used, the emphasis at an assessment centre is on the observable behaviour of candidates, and to that end the exercises will have been designed to capture and simulate key aspects of the relevant job. The candidates' – your – performance on the chosen tasks will then be assessed against criteria derived from the competencies required for the job.

Unfortunately, many good candidates fail to do themselves justice because they are unaware of the kinds of tasks they may be asked to undertake when attending an assessment centre.

The aims of this book, therefore, are to:

● inform you about what to expect when you are asked to attend for extended assessment;
● explain how such assessments are conducted and how this fits into the whole recruitment and selection process;
● offer advice on how you should behave during your time at an assessment centre in both formal and informal situations;
● give guidance on how you might prepare for different forms of assessment (including ability and other tests) in order to maximize your chances of success;
● suggest learning activities that you can undertake in order to prepare yourself for the different types of assessment exercises you are likely to face.

Chapter 1

Assessment centres

The aims of this chapter are to explain:

- what an assessment centre is;
- what kind of programme to expect;
- the assessment exercises you are likely to encounter;
- how to cope with the demands that will be placed upon you;
- how you might prepare yourself for an assessment centre.

What exactly is an assessment centre?

If you are invited to attend an assessment centre as part of the selection procedures for a job, promotion or further training, you will probably join a small group of six to eight other applicants. At the centre you will be asked to undertake a series of assessments that have been designed to reveal to the assessors whether or not you possess the personal competencies and technical skills necessary for you to work effectively in the relevant job or to benefit from further training.

Depending on the arrangements, the assessment process can

take anything from a few hours to a couple of days. In the latter case both the candidates and the assessors are likely to be in residence at the same place. It is not surprising, therefore, that some candidates find this to be quite stressful, not least because they are in an unfamiliar environment with people they don't know. In addition, they may well feel that they cannot relax because their perception is that they are being assessed at all times – even at break times and social events within the programme. However, you should bear in mind that getting groups of applicants together in this way is expensive. Consequently, organizations cannot afford to invite large numbers of candidates to an assessment centre. So, it is worth remembering that, if you get through to this stage in the recruit-ment–selection process, you must be close to being one of the chosen candidates. If you are not yet on the 'shortlist' of those from whom the final selection will be made, you are certainly on the 'longlist'.

What to expect at an assessment centre – the programme

So, if you are fortunate enough to receive an invitation to attend an assessment centre what should you expect? The letter inviting you to attend should give you a good idea. For example, it should provide you with details concerning the venue itself – the address, location and how to get there. You should also be given some preliminary information about the assessment centre itself, including an outline of the programme, together with an approximate schedule. Under normal circumstances you should also be given an indication of the types of assess-ment that will be used and their place and purpose in the overall selection process. Some employers may even send you some sample test items as an aid to your preparation together with a questionnaire to complete.

What this information should also signal to you is that the programme at an assessment centre is both highly organized and tightly structured. This can be illustrated by reference to the sample timetables given in Figure1.1 and Figure 1.2.

```
10.00      Arrive, registration, coffee
10.15      Welcome and introductions
10.30      Cognitive and personality tests
12.30      Buffet lunch with departmental staff
13.45      Panel interviews*
15.00      Break
15.15      Group discussion exercise
16.30      Debriefing
17.00      Depart

*Applicants who do not do well on the tests may be asked to leave
following a short feedback session
```

Figure 1.1   Sample timetable for a one-day assessment centre

These sample timetables are intended to show what you might expect if you are invited to a one-day or a two-day assessment centre respectively – although when studying these you need to bear in mind that there are no hard-and-fast rules about how such programmes should be compiled. Consequently, there are many variants depending upon the circumstances. So, if you want to know exactly what to expect, you will need to take a careful look at the programme for the particular assessment centre you have been invited to attend.

What the two sample timetables also show is how busy you can expect to be during the time when you are at an assessment centre. Indeed, as a candidate, you will find that there will be

Day 1	
17.00	Arrive at venue for the assessment centre (for example, a hotel)
18.00	Welcome and introductory briefing
18.30	Icebreaker activity
20.00	Dinner with representatives from the organization and assessors

Work on preparatory task for the following day's activities (for example, complete a questionnaire, read documents provided)

Day 2	
09.00	Introduction to the day's programme
09.15	Cognitive test and personality inventory
11.00	Coffee
11.15	In-tray exercise
12.15	Presentations
13.00	Lunch with senior managers and assessors
14.00	Group decision-making exercise
15.00	Break
15.15	Interviews
16.15	Debriefing session and brief presentation of the organization's training and development programme
17.00	Finish and depart

Figure 1.2   Sample timetable for a two-day assessment centre

very little time when you are not actively engaged in one form of assessment or another. All of this variety and intensity of activity is intended to do more than simply provide the assessors with as much evidence as possible about the applicants in the shortest possible time. Part of its purpose is to observe at first hand how you behave under pressure by simulating the circumstances under which you might be expected to perform in a real workplace. In turn, the variety of assessment tasks is intended to provide different forms of evaluation evidence about you and the other candidates. This will then enable the assessors to build up a profile of each candidate based on her or his performance on the individual assessment items. The completed profiles can then be used when making the final decision. In short, the defining principle of an assessment centre is that it should be multi-task, multi-assessor and multi-context. In this way objectivity and reliability of the result is secured.

What to expect at an assessment centre – the assessment activities

As with the programme, there is no set formula as to how many exercises, or which combination of activities, should be included in an assessment centre. This is because the assessment tasks will have been chosen to provide the assessors with evidence of the extent to which the candidates possess those competencies judged to be relevant to the particular job or development opportunity under consideration. However, the research findings that are summarized in Table 1.1 tell us that certain types of exercise are more likely to occur at an assessment centre than others, irrespective of the size of the recruiting organization.

For example, as Table 1.1 shows, it is almost certain to include some form of interview (a one-to-one interview, perhaps, or with an interview panel). There is also a very high probability that it will include, in descending order, some form of aptitude (ability) test, personality test and a group discussion exercise of some kind or other. In addition, there is a good chance that it will involve a case study, a presentation and in-tray exercises. Consequently, you should expect to find some combination of the following activities as part of an assessment centre programme:

Table 1.1   Content of assessment centre exercises in the UK according to size of recruiting organizations (small, medium, large)

Type of exercise	Small (%)	Medium (%)	Large (%)	Total sample (%)
Interview	97	97	97	97
Aptitude test	89	91	91	91
Personality test	80	83	79	80
Group discussion	67	79	89	79
Case study	49	64	71	62
Presentation	54	59	61	58
In-tray	19	38	48	35

Source: Keenan, T (1995) Graduate recruitment in Britain: A survey of selection methods used by organizations, *Journal of Organizational Behaviour*, 16, pp 303–17

- one-to-one-interviews and panel interviews;
- ability tests (sometimes known as 'cognitive' or 'psychometric' tests);
- personality tests (or 'inventories');
- group discussion exercises;
- case studies;
- in-tray exercises;
- presentations.

So, what exactly is involved in each of these assessment activities? By way of giving you an overview, brief descriptions of the most common types of exercise are provided below. More detailed guidance on what is involved, and what preparation you can do, is given in the subsequent chapters of this book.

Interviews

As Table 1.1 shows, if the research is anything to go by, one thing you can be certain of is that the vast majority of assessment centres include an interview of some kind. It may well be that this holds no fears for you – indeed you may already have had an interview prior to your receiving an invitation to attend an assessment centre. However, you would be well advised to approach this so-called 'second interview' with greater care and prepare for it even more thoroughly. This is not just because the stakes are getting higher the closer you get to the point at which the final selection is made – second interviews tend to be more challenging.

So, in what ways do assessment centre interviews differ from first interviews? The main features of second interviews are:

- often conducted by a panel drawn from senior managers, staff with relevant professional or technical expertise, human resource personnel and outside consultants;
- driven by specific selection criteria, and as such provide evidence that complements information obtained by other means;
- highly focused and with more searching questions, which might be informed by how you have performed on the other assessment exercises;
- likely to focus at some point on any issues and problems raised in your first interview that need further exploration.

In the light of this knowledge it is worth doing a little preparation before you go to the assessment centre. As you can see from the sample timetables above, the chances are that you will not have the time when you get there. A checklist of useful things that you can do to start that process is given in Figure 1.3.

To sum up, expect your assessment centre interview to be more demanding than the one that helped to get you there,

---

You can prepare in advance for your assessment centre interview by:

✓ taking a careful look at the job details together with your initial application, CV and covering letter and reflecting on them in the light of the knowledge you have since gained;

✓ studying any notes you made following your first interview;

✓ thinking about what questions you were asked at that interview and whether or not any areas were left unexplored;

✓ trying to identify what new questions you might be asked or areas the interviewers might wish to explore;

✓ gathering relevant information about the organization, for example from someone you know who may have had a second interview or via the Internet.

Figure 1.3 Advance preparation checklist for assessment-centre interviews

make sure you are familiar with what you said in your application form and CV, and find out as much as you can about the job and the organization. More detailed guidance is given in Chapter 5.

Ability tests

The use of tests in personnel selection is based on the assumption that there are stable job-related differences between candidates and that these differences can be measured with a sufficient degree of accuracy to be of value to employers. The ability tests chosen for use at an assessment centre, therefore, will have been specifically designed to assess how good people are at certain things. So, expect to be given a test or tests that will provide the assessors with some objective evidence of what you are able to do – in other words your aptitude.

The most commonly used ability tests are designed to measure your skills in numeracy and verbal reasoning. There are also tests that can be used to assess problem solving, technical, and spatial reasoning skills. Hence any cognitive tests that are used at an assessment centre will have been carefully chosen to provide evidence of the skills and abilities relevant to the job under consideration. That evidence will then be considered alongside the outcomes from the other assessment exercises in arriving at the final selection. The beauty of an assessment centre is that the result does not depend solely on one exercise, unlike an interview.

The most common features of ability tests are that:

- they invariably begin with one or two worked examples to introduce you to what is involved and inform you about how to proceed;
- there are strict time limits for each test, designed in such a way as to put you under time pressure – so much so that you may not be able to complete all of the questions;
- the answers to the items will be either right or wrong;
- there is a tendency for the items to be arranged on a 'gradient of difficulty', with the easiest questions at the beginning and the hardest at the end;
- they may be in the form of a 'paper-and-pencil test' or candidates may be asked to complete them online.

To sum up, nearly all recruiters make use of some form of ability test at an assessment centre in order to measure the aptitude of candidates. The choice of which tests are used will be closely related to the abilities judged to be relevant to the job on offer. More detailed guidance is provided in Chapter 4.

Personality tests

Personality tests, sometimes called 'personality inventories', are designed to measure personality characteristics or 'traits' such as your motivation to work, how you interact with other people, and how you deal with your emotions. Information of this kind is of great interest to prospective employers as a basis for predicting how your personality is likely to affect your performance at work. It may be important, for example, for them to know if you are the kind of person who can stay calm but alert in the conditions that prevail in a particular work-place, or have the ability to adapt to the culture of the organization. Evidence from personality tests, along with that derived from ability tests and other forms of assessment, therefore, are used to help employers choose the people they think are best suited for the job or would benefit most from further training. The common features of personality tests are as follows:

● as with ability tests they start with one or two sample items to give you an idea as to what is involved and how to proceed;
● although time pressure is less important than it is with ability tests, you will usually be given a fixed time to complete the inventory;
● unlike ability tests there are no right or wrong answers;
● they usually include some items that check whether or not you are trying to give a false impression of yourself by answering dishonestly and inconsistently;
● they may be in 'paper-and-pencil' form or you may be required to complete them online;
● the answers are used to construct an individual personality profile.

To sum up, you should expect your personality to be assessed in some way or another. To that end it will help if you know yourself well, are prepared to be honest, and are aware of the qualities the job requires. More detailed guidance is given in Chapter 4.

Group exercises

Group exercises require you to interact with others in prearranged ways in order that the assessors can observe and assess your behaviour. The group exercises used at an assessment centre fall into three main categories: group discussions; problem solving and team games. Discussion groups include:

● leaderless discussion, in which all of the participants are given the same brief and are expected to work towards achieving a consensus;
● discussions in which each member of the group is given the opportunity (for example, 10 minutes) to chair the proceedings;
● discussion, in which each of the participants is presented with a different brief, assigning them a role that they are expected to play in the subsequent interactions of the group.

In the case of problem-solving exercises, you should expect to be given a task that requires your group to work together to find a solution to a problem. This can take the form of an abstract problem, or be based on case study material (see below) that requires decision making based on concrete material derived from a specific context, which may be either real or hypothetical.

Team games are the final variant of group exercises. Typically, you will be a member of a team that is given a common task to complete in competition with another team or against the clock. It is very common in exercises such as these for the group to be given a collection of basic materials such as newspaper, string and sticky tape, or a construction kit, which they are instructed to use to build items such as a tower, or a bridge. Under this heading you should also be prepared for role-playing exercises in which you may be asked to act the part of a character, usually in a work-related context.

In exercises such as these the assessors will be looking for behavioural evidence of your:

● ability to participate in the group's activities and to make a positive contribution to achieving its goals;
● oral communication skills including your ability to present reasoned arguments;
● listening skills;
● negotiation skills and assertiveness;
● ability to work effectively with others – including your interpersonal skills;
● leadership skills.

To sum up, there is a very good chance that you will be involved in some form of group discussion activity at an assessment centre, especially those run on behalf of large organizations. You should expect these to take many different forms, but in each case it will be your observable behaviour that will be of interest to the assessors. For further guidance see Chapter 2 and Chapter 6.

Case study

The most common form of a case study used at assessment

centres involves a business or technical problem that has been chosen because it is both realistic and relevant to the job on offer. You might well be given a set of documents relevant to the problem and be required to work with others in a group. In such cases the exercise will be a variant of the group exercises described above. As such it may be that it is not the solution to the problem that will be of interest to the assessors but how it was arrived at and hence your contribution to that process. Thus, a case study is normally used as a vehicle for generating a wide range of activities in order to provide the assessors with evidence of your oral communication and teamworking skills as well as your ability to:

● analyse issues embedded in the case study material;
● interpret data presented in a variety of forms;
● consider alternative solutions to the problem posed;
● produce a written report setting out solutions and making recommendations.

To sum up, case studies tend to be more popular with large recruiters. They are usually focused on a real or imaginary problem that is used to generate a wide range of individual and group activities. For further guidance see Chapter 6.

Presentations

Increasingly, employers across all occupational sectors are seeking to recruit employees with good oral communication skills – very few job roles now escape this requirement. Hence, during an assessment centre, you will be placed in a variety of situations (interviews, group discussion and presentations) in which you are required to deploy those skills.

Any number of different approaches can be adopted in

presentation exercises. For example, you could be asked to give a short 15-minute presentation on a given subject. You might be given advance notice of this, in which case you would have a chance to do some preparation. On the other hand you could be 'thrown in at the deep end' with little or no time to prepare what you want to say and how best to say it – a good test of your ability to 'think on your feet'. In other circumstances, you might be asked to analyse some case study material, such as information relating to a particular problem, and to use that as the basis for your presentation, which might take the form of a proposed solution to the problem. Clearly, the presentation will provide the assessors with evidence of your knowledge and understanding of the topic under consideration as well as your ability to:

- think logically in order to structure the content of your presentation;
- deploy information in such a way as to make a case or advance an argument;
- speak clearly and audibly to an audience;
- use language (including technical terminology or 'jargon') appropriately;
- use the overhead projector or ICT facilities with skill;
- handle stress and appear self-confident under pressure.

To sum up, there is a strong possibility that your oral communication skills (including your ability to give an effective presentation) will come under close scrutiny at an assessment centre. The means by which this is done, and the contexts in which it occurs, can vary between assessment centres. Nevertheless, you should be prepared for it to happen at some stage – perhaps within the framework of a wider assessment exercise such as a case study. For more detailed guidance see Chapter 3.

In-tray exercises

With an in-tray exercise candidates are usually asked to adopt a particular role as an employee in a fictitious organization and to deal with the contents of an imaginary in-tray. Typically, this consists of a sample of internal memos, letters, e-mails, faxes, phone messages and reports. These items will have been chosen to ensure that they vary in their importance, complexity and urgency. The precise details of the task may vary from one assessment centre to another but you will probably be asked to respond in writing to each item in the in-tray and to make a note of the reasons behind your chosen course of action in every case. Such exercises are often given a greater sense of reality by the inclusion of a developing crisis or problem that the candidate is expected to resolve whilst dealing with the other items in the in-tray. To add to the pressure, new items (an urgent fax or an e-mail) may be introduced during the exercise. Clearly, exercises such as this will provide the assessors with evidence of your ability to:

- analyse and solve problems;
- organize and prioritize tasks under pressure;
- delegate tasks to others;
- manage the use of time;
- read quickly and efficiently;
- write effectively.

To sum up, in-tray exercises are an attempt to simulate the conditions you might be expected to encounter in a real workplace in order to observe how well you can cope. As such they provide the assessors with a wide range of first-hand evidence about the candidate and their ability. More detailed guidance is given in Chapter 6.

How will your performance be assessed?

The important thing to remember about how you will be assessed at an assessment centre is that a variety of methods will be used to gather information about you. Hence, there is no single way in which your performance will be judged. For example, the method used to mark your answers in an ability test will be very different from that used to assess your performance on a group discussion exercise. After you have taken the test, your paper will be marked objectively, perhaps electronically, to produce a total score. The assessors will already have determined what the minimum score (or 'pass mark') should be for each particular selection exercise. They may have decided, for example, that a high score has to be achieved on one of the tests because it will provide an accurate measure of your ability in an area of competence (such as numeracy) considered to be essential for the appointment they are seeking to make. Indeed, in some cases it may not be possible for candidates to compensate for a low mark on that one component by their performance on the other exercises.

By comparison, the observation methods used to assess your performance on many of the other exercises will appear to be more subjective. However, particular care will have been taken to make sure that the assessors' judgements are both valid and reliable. With regard to the former, this will be achieved by basing their judgements on assessment criteria derived from a careful analysis of the requirements of the job. In respect of the latter, the use of agreed criteria also increases the reliability of assessment by ensuring that the assessors are all looking for the same things. This will be reinforced by the fact that, from time to time, they will cross-check their judgements in order to eliminate variations in assessment from one assessor to another.

They will be aided in this process by the record sheets that they use to rate the candidates' performance on the different exercises. So, you will always be able to tell who the assessors are – they will be the ones holding clipboards and making careful notes!

The assessors will probably use a master sheet to record your scores on each activity, and so build up a profile of the strengths and weaknesses of each individual. It will be on the basis of this evidence that the final selection will be made.

Social activities and events

If you take another look at the sample schedules (Figure 1.1 and Figure 1.2) it will not escape your notice that, in addition to the time that is devoted to tests and assessment exercises, candidates are expected to participate in some form of social activity or event. This may well consist of no more than a buffet lunch at which you will have an opportunity to meet and talk informally to different people – fellow candidates, recent entrants to the organization, managers and assessors. Time may also have been set aside for a site visit and meetings with representatives from the organization other than those involved in the assessment centre. Please bear in mind that these are not just 'time-fillers' – they will have been structured into the programme quite deliberately. As such they will give you an opportunity to unwind a little, and to ask questions about the job and the organization including the wider context in which it operates (such as its business environment).

So, don't be lulled into thinking that these activities and events are so unimportant that you can afford to just relax and 'let your hair down'. Indeed, someone may be waiting to catch you off your guard before asking you a searching question.

Hence, you would be well advised on occasions such as these to show that you are socially aware and sensitive to the needs of the situation by:

- being willing to mix and engage in polite conversation with those who are present;
- communicating through your actions that you are interested and alert (for example, by listening and responding to what others are saying);
- being polite, courteous and sociable to everyone you meet irrespective of their status;
- watching your intake of alcohol and not allowing yourself to become too informal with those present, including the other candidates.

To sum up, there will be opportunities at the assessment centre to socialize – over coffee, at mealtimes and during breaks. You should remember that these provide the assessors with a chance to see how well you can mix with others in such contexts. At the same time they give you an opportunity to find out more about the job and the organization and to show that you are socially adept.

Punctuality

Punctuality is getting where you have to be on time every time. Getting there on time shouldn't be a problem once you have arrived at the assessment centre. But you could still arrive at a room late for one of the activities – for example, your interview. Hard as it might be to believe, it does happen and when it does it is a great source of irritation because, as you can see from the sample timetables provided above, assessment centres are always run to a very tight schedule. Do it once and your behaviour may appear to have gone unnoticed; do it more than once and it certainly will not!

Dress code

Be warned – there are still employers around who say things like 'The first points I look for are a good handshake and clean shoes. For me, a limp handshake is an immediate negative.' So you had better firm up those handshakes, avoid fidgeting and remember to make eye contact with the interviewers. Seriously, first impressions do last and are very important. Put yourself in the interviewers' shoes – what would you like to see when you first meet a candidate?

What you wear might well be a matter that is taken out of your hands to a degree if a dress code is in force at the assessment centre. However, beware of the dreaded term 'smart casual' – especially you males. Experience suggests that women are more likely to err on the 'smart' side of the injunction. Males on the other hand have a tendency to seize on the 'casual' at the expense of the 'smart' and turn up in jeans and maybe even a tee shirt as well. Probably, the safest course of action is to wear a suit – after all you can usually manage to shed the jacket (and the tie) most of the time so that very quickly the 'smart' can become 'casual' and vice versa.

The key points to bear in mind are:

- if you have any doubts about the dress code check it out in advance;
- make certain you are smart and tidy – the interviewers will see this as a reflection of you and your attitudes;

- don't wear overbearing perfume or aftershave – you don't want the interviewers to remember you as the one who gave them a headache;
- make sure you are comfortable with what you wear – you will be less self-conscious and more self-confident if you are;
- the way you look should show how you think and feel about yourself – so be positive.

How to prepare for an assessment centre

It would be easy to adopt the attitude that, unlike an examination, you cannot study for an assessment centre or that it is better just to 'trust to luck'. In our view, nothing could be further from the truth – hence this book. So here is a checklist of ideas to help you to prepare for, and do your best at, an assessment centre:

- Forget the idea that you cannot prepare for an assessment centre – there are many sensible things that you can do to help your cause if you are prepared to make the effort.
- If you have had some previous experience with ability tests and personality inventories it will be to your advantage – as you will find out in Chapter 4, there are plenty of books of practice tests you can use.
- Adopt a positive mental attitude towards both your preparation and attendance at the assessment centre itself.
- If you are given any preparatory information or materials make certain that you read them carefully in advance.
- Take another look at the job description and any information you were given about the organization to see if they give any clues as to the type of employee they are

seeking or the questions you might be asked in an inter-view.

- Try to ensure that you arrive at the assessment centre as relaxed and well rested as you can – it can be a very exacting and tiring experience and you will need to have all your wits about you.
- Gather as much 'intelligence' as you can about assessment centres, for example by talking to friends and acquaintances who have attended one in order to find out about what was expected of them and how they coped with its demands.
- Try to be yourself by acting as naturally as you can – don't try to manipulate the impression that you give.
- Undertake a review or audit of your prior experience to date (for example, as a student or in previous employment) in order to identify what you have learned that is relevant to the job for which you have applied and on which you would like to build as part of your personal development plan.
- If you think that you have not performed well in a particular assessment, try not to let this have an adverse impact on your performance on the other exercises – you may not have done as badly as you think and it may well be that your performance overall will be more important.
- See the assessment centre as a two-way process where the employer can find out more about you as a prospective employee, and where you can find out about the organiza-tion and the job for which you have applied.
- Think of the assessment centre not just as a means of getting a job but as an opportunity to have a valuable learning experience at someone else's expense.

You can start this process by working your way through the rest of this book and by following the advice and guidance provided in the individual chapters. You can also undertake an audit of your personal skills using the framework provided in Appendix 1. Good luck with both your preparation and your experiences at an assessment centre.

Chapter 2

How to succeed in group exercises

The purpose of this chapter is to acquaint you with the different types of group exercises that you might encounter at an assessment centre including activities known as 'icebreakers' and those involving group discussion. It also provides you with guidance on how to function effectively in such activities including the assessment criteria used by assessors, making contributions to group processes, completing tasks, and knowing when and how to negotiate and to compromise. Above all, the aim is to help you prepare for group exercises both before and at the assessment centre.

Why are group exercises used in the selection process?

Group exercises are used by recruiters and others because they provide evidence that is difficult to obtain by any other method. For example, they enable people to be assessed while interacting with each other, and allow candidates to reveal characteristics of which they themselves may not be fully aware, such as cutting across others or holding back when they should be contributing. Above all, they provide a lot of evidence in a short time of actual, not reported, behaviour.

Critics of group exercises say that they reward those with the 'gift of the gab', but 'gab' is not such a great thing, especially if it consists of empty platitudes or talk for its own sake. The assessors do not reward that. But do not despise fluency or longer interventions because you think they will draw attention to yourself. That, after all, is the point – the assessors, and particularly your assessor, want to be able to see and hear you. Once 'on air', the best thing you can do is speak easily and to the point, taking care to carry the discussion forward. If, as happens all too often in life, someone is 'hogging' the discussion, it is up to you, perhaps working with others, to act, courteously but firmly, in order to get that person 'off air'. Your assessors will notice your actions and reward you accordingly.

While obviously they can never be entirely 'true to life', group exercises have enough going in their favour to make their inclusion in an assessment centre worthwhile or even essential. Firstly, they are fair because they give everyone the same opportunity, under the same conditions, to show how they can function as members of a group. Secondly, they do not usually require any particular specialist knowledge. Consequently, people from different backgrounds can contribute with equal effectiveness providing – and under some circumstances this is an important issue – that the standard of their spoken English is adequate for the purpose.

So, in order to do your best, you need to remember the following points:

● be yourself – do not try to project a 'different' image;
● the quality of what you say is more important than the quantity – don't talk just for the sake of it, but do talk;

- if you say nothing, you are missing an opportunity to demonstrate your strengths – so try to make as positive a contribution to the discussion as you can;
- people with very different styles can perform with equal effectiveness – it is not a competition to see who can dominate the group.

What are the assessors looking for?

First, a word about assessors. You may not like it, but you simply have to accept their presence in the room. However unobtrusive they try to be, you will still be aware of their presence. In particular, you will notice that one of them is sitting opposite you, maybe not directly opposite, but opposite enough for you to recognize that this is your assessor. Having registered that fact, the best thing you can do is to forget about him or her. Above all, do not try to: establish eye contact with the assessor; address your remarks to the assessor; look at the assessor when someone says something with which you do not agree or when the progress of the group takes a turn for the worse. Such behaviour only signals to the assessor that you are 'putting on a show' for his or her benefit, or that you lack confidence in what you are saying and that you are beginning to panic. None of these behaviours will be to your advantage.

The sort of questions the assessors will be asking when they observe your behaviour are as follows:

- Can you help the group to achieve its objectives by identifying ways of tackling the problem?
- Can you 'think on your feet' and speak effectively in front of others?
- Can you inject some structure into the discussion to help the group to shape up its response?

- Can you build on what others say in order to broaden and deepen the collective attack on the problem?
- Can you get the best out of the group by drawing others into the discussion, or by challenging those who are wasting the group's time by talking off the point?
- Can you drive the group to completion of its tasks?

The likelihood is that your assessors will also be looking for evidence that you possess, or have the potential to develop, competence in the following areas:

- interpersonal ('people') skills;
- leadership;
- communication;
- focus on results: goal-orientation and achievement drive;
- working with others – 'teamwork'.

How strong do you think you are in relation to competencies such as these? If you are uncertain, or even if you are certain, take a little time to complete a few of the self-audits provided in Appendix 1 at the end of this book. The results should give you an indication of your strengths and weaknesses, and hence what you need to work on as part of your preparation for your attendance at an assessment centre.

When evaluating performance in group exercises, assessors typically work to a set of indicators. Sometimes these can be wholly positive and wholly negative. The set given in Figure 2.1 for 'Teamwork' is intended to give you an idea of what these performance indicators look like, although in practice there would be a few more. Notice that each indicator A to E is given a rating between 1 and 7 (only 1 and 7 are shown here) before an overall rating is determined. This is not necessarily an arithmetical average, but a weighing up arrived at by studying or 'eyeballing' the distribution of scores.

A	Treats people with courtesy and respect at all times	7
	Shows no courtesy or respect	1
B	Shows interest in what others have to say	7
	Shows no interest in what others have to say	1
C	Contributes ideas freely and openly	7
	Keeps ideas, if any, under wraps	1
D	Offers non-verbal support to others	7
	Withholds non-verbal support	1
E	Tries to understand where others are coming from	7
	Makes no effort to understand where others are coming from	1
Key points of performance:		
What was done well?		
What could have been done better?		
Overall rating	7 6 5 4 3 2 1	

Figure 2.1 Performance indicators used to assess teamwork

Of course, you do not have to be a 'gung-ho' team player, or pretend to be one – employers do not expect that in everyone, or even in most of their employees. However, since they have gone to the trouble of including teamwork as a desirable competency, the least they expect is a recognition that there is a team ethic and a willingness to suppress ego in the wider interests of the organization. In short, what they will be looking for, in situations such as this, is evidence of your ability to 'fit in' with other employees.

In group discussion exercises, individualists who are pursuing their own agenda are pretty easy to spot. For example, when someone prefaces an intervention with 'From my point of view...', or 'It seems to me that...', or 'As I said before...', you can be sure that they are thinking of themselves and not of the group and its task. Remember, if you persist in repeating a point of view over and over again the assessors will simply write 'repetitive' in their notes.

Again, employers do not expect everyone or even most of the candidates to be driven, 'can-do' obsessives. What they are looking out for, via the assessors, are people who are capable of buckling down to tackle a problem within strict time constraints. In these circumstances, assessors often hear the complaint 'It wouldn't be like that in real life – we would have far longer to do that.' However, you should keep in mind that employers don't want to hear whingeing of that kind (or indeed of any kind), so even if you think the task is unrealistic do not say it. Take the task at face value and try hard to solve the problem by working as constructively as you can with the others in your group.

Assigned, non-assigned and assumed roles

Basically, there are three types of group discussion:

- *Assigned roles* in which people are given different working briefs – some of the elements will be common to all and some will be assigned to individuals.
- *Non-assigned roles* in which all members of the group are given the same brief.
- *Assumed roles* in which there is no working brief provided – people assume roles by virtue of previous work experi-

ences that they take into the exercise. Typically, this is based on the discussion of an issue that has been the subject of a presentation.

Assigned roles

The advantages of assigned roles are that they:

- lend themselves to more realistic scenarios;
- allow better assessment of some competencies like fact finding and negotiation;
- give everyone a more even chance to contribute.

The last point means that no one has an excuse for not contributing so it becomes easier for an assessor to recognize underperformance on the part of a candidate. The downside of assigned roles exercises is that you may be given a role with which you feel uncomfortable. If so, just accept it as part of the challenge, and the likelihood is that others in the group are in the same boat.

The smartest way to treat an assigned role – whether you like it or not – is to try to do justice to the role but not to allow yourself to get stuck in it. Once you have succeeded in negotiating or otherwise agreeing what you would regard as the sticking points of your brief (or giving way gracefully under superior reasoning and persuasion) you are free to work towards the best solution of the problem from the organization's point of view. After all, in real life no one would be expected to go on arguing a narrow functional brief.

Non-assigned roles

The advantage of a group exercise with non-assigned roles –

and it is considerable – is that it allows a leader to emerge. The same applies to assumed roles. Remember, however, that there is no reason why a leader should not emerge from a group exercise in which the roles have been assigned.

Assumed roles

If you are asked to attend a group discussion and to begin by giving a five-minute prepared presentation, which is then followed by open discussion once everyone has given their presentation, you are being asked to take on an assumed role. Your role is, then, to argue your corner based on what you have said, but to be prepared to give way or support another solution if that is the way the discussion goes. In that sense, you are only playing yourself. The virtue of this you might think is that you are not saddled with what you might regard as an artificial or unwanted brief. That said, you still have to get to grips with issues that might be alien to you and come up with something sensible to say, especially in your presentation.

Tactical considerations

When in a group discussion there are some tactical dimensions of which you should be aware. These are related to the positions people may come to occupy in the group and their inner motivation.

There are two major positions and one that is of minor importance. The major positions are chair and scribe; the minor one is that of timekeeper, which either the chair or the scribe can usually do as part of their wider role.

It is easy to think that being the chair or scribe (especially the former) would give you an advantage, not least because it would give you the opportunity to do a lot of the talking, which would then put you in the limelight. Sometimes groups believe so strongly in the advantages conferred on the person who becomes the chair (although without vocalizing it to each other) that they refuse to appoint one, usually with dire consequences.

The role of the scribe is not usually seen as being so advantageous because of the nature of the work it involves. However, if you take it you are potentially in a position to influence the group, if not command it. So it is worth taking a look in more detail at the three positions.

Chair

If you are tempted by the prospect of being the chair make sure that you can do the job before you volunteer, or allow yourself to be nominated. This is because being the chair carries a tariff with it: do it well and you can benefit in how you are assessed; do it badly and you can lose out, notably to whoever tries to salvage something from the wreckage you have helped to create. The best advice, therefore, is to be careful if someone tries to flatter you into taking on the job – for example, by saying 'You look as if you know what you are doing, so you be chair.' If you don't take care, before you know where you are, you may find yourself running (or trying to run) the meeting. After all, the chances are that you will hardly know the people you are working with, so why respond to their flattery, especially if it is not in your best interests to do so.

A good chair directs the traffic, makes sure that everyone is brought into the discussion, facilitates the process by making timely interventions, curtails rambling, and generally moves things along towards the achievement of an agreed outcome. The chair does not have to do all those things because there must be room for others to take appropriate action, but in essence that is the job description. If you do not feel confident about carrying out responsibilities such as these, don't volunteer or allow yourself to be pressured into accepting someone else's nomination. An assessment centre is not the place to experiment if in doing so you are likely to display your weaknesses.

On balance it is much better to have a chair than to try to proceed without one. After all, if the person you select turns out to be hopeless, then the group can quickly drop him or her and you are all no worse off than you were before. Observation of chairless groups shows that they are usually rambling, directionless and low on energy. So, unless the people in a group know what they are doing, and the chances are that a scratch group like the one you will be involved in will not, the advice is to co-operate in the selection of a chair.

Wilfully not nominating a chair is really a defensive ploy designed to ensure that no one benefits too much from the exercise – better we all score 4/10 than someone scores 8/10, or so the reasoning goes. It is a line of thinking that could be very dangerous. For example, unbeknown to you the assessors may be operating a 'hurdles policy' whereby all successful candidates are required to reach a minimum score on every exercise. Hence, you could be blowing your own chances at the outset of the exercise by colluding with the rest of the group in making such a decision.

Scribe

There is a poisoned chalice element to being the scribe, but then there are risks attached to any decision you might make to turn down or refuse to volunteer for a job. With the scribe the trick is to serve the group with a solid contribution, but not to spend too long on the flipchart (for invariably it is a flipchart). Again, be careful not to allow yourself to be lured into the job. Given that there are always people who will say 'my hand-writing is hopeless' or words to that effect, you might, if you believe your handwriting is better than that, react by putting up your hand to volunteer your services.

Mind you, the opportunity may already have gone - there is usually no shortage of people wanting to grab the pen. They do this because they think it will give them visibility and the chance to shape the group's outcome. They are right to think this but it is a long way between thought and execution. Just as with the chair, you have to have a good idea what you are doing, and you need to know when to stop. Staying on the flipchart all the way through is invariably a bad idea. More on that later.

Just as with chair, if you want to be scribe you had better be confident you can do the job well. To be an effective scribe you actually do need clear handwriting, but that is only the begin-ning. What really matters is a sense of structure; the material you produce has to be organized into something that ideally is self-standing. This means that anyone could go to the flipchart after the group has left and the contents would make sense. Experience suggests that the ability to do this is far from common. So if you become the scribe make sure the group gives you a structure and use it right from the start. Remember, the worst thing that you can do is to write down everything the group members offer as it comes without processing it first. If you do that, all you will have to show for your efforts will be an incoherent laundry list.

The next hazard is to avoid falling in love with your creation. It is all too easy to stop and admire and titivate what you have written while the rest of the group goes on talking. An extension of this is when you start adding material of your own devising. How often have we seen scribes scribbling away with their backs to the group? This is definitely bad. Remember, you are there to reflect and perhaps express the thoughts of the group, which of course includes yourself. You are not there to write up your version of how the set task should be resolved.

Now to why you should not glue yourself to the flipchart. It is not a matter of overstaying your welcome: the group will probably be quite happy for you to continue. Should you put the pen down someone may even hand it back to you to indicate that you should keep going. Standing down is in your own interests. Think about it – what is most difficult to do while writing and (hopefully) structuring and processing? It is contributing meaningfully to the discussion. Some people can do both, but it is a tough call. Better to do your bit as scribe and then stand down gracefully, taking care as you do to find a form of words more winning than 'could someone else take over now?' There ought to be someone ready. After all, if scribes should contribute to the discussion then other contributors should scribe. So you should find that one of the more aware members of the group, having done some contributing, is keen or at least willing to take over as scribe.

Sometimes groups jump too readily into appointing a scribe, as if it were a safety blanket. The danger, as with the positions of chair and timekeeper, is that if you get someone else to do the work you don't have to do it yourself – you can forget about it. Isn't it preferable for members of the group to keep their own notes and then, when the time is ripe, collectively convert them into a summary, at which point a scribe becomes necessary?

Timekeeper

Having someone keep the time is necessary, but not sufficient, to make sure the group finishes in time. It is all very well bawling out the time but if the group isn't making headway with the task there is little point. Better to shout out the time and make some positive suggestion as to how things should be moved forward. If you like, it is timekeeper as enforcer. But isn't that the chair's job? In reality everyone should be their own timekeeper: it is not so difficult keeping track of the time, especially if there is a clock in the room as there should be.

So, do not expect to pick up many 'brownie points' from the assessors by being the timekeeper unless, as indicated above, you do something else too. If you are going to be the time-keeper, make sure that you get it right. Amazing as it may sound, it is not unknown for a timekeeper to call out the wrong time and in so doing be in danger of seriously misleading the group if other members are not alert to the situation.

The icebreaker

The icebreaker or warm-up exercise is intended to do just that: break the ice among participants and generally warm up the proceedings, the supposition being that everyone is nervous or a bit 'uptight'. These routines vary from the perfunctory to the elaborate.

Examples of icebreakers

An example of a perfunctory icebreaker would be just going round the table in turns saying who you are to the rest of the group. The next step would be to tell the group three things about yourself that no one sitting at the table would be expected to know, including an unfulfilled ambition. There is obviously scope for humour and boasting here, which the 'show-offs' will usually grasp. But it is harmless fun and it really does not matter if you don't believe that someone pushed a pea up Mount Everest with their nose, or wants to cross the Atlantic on a beermat. The main thing is that it starts you talking and stirs the adrenalin, which is the purpose of the exercise. Notice that this is not strictly a group exercise but an individual activity done with a group acting as the audience.

Where the activities at an assessment centre are based on a running scenario involving a fictitious organization you may find that an icebreaker exercise is used to help you get inside that organization. Thus if the organization is called 'As You Like It Leisure' and you have applied for a real job in the marketing department, you may well be given a background document containing relevant information and be asked to explore it with one or more of the other members of the group. For such a task where people work in pairs, the instructions might well be like those given in Figure 2.2.

Using the icebreaker to acclimatize

Icebreakers, like the exercise described above, pose a gentle challenge, but as they will always be non-assessed you have nothing to fear. Use them as an opportunity to find your feet in the assessment centre and to prepare yourself for the sterner tests to follow.

Actors or professional role players

Group exercises can involve some role play other than the role play involved in following an assigned brief. It is becoming quite commonplace for actors or professional role players to be introduced into group exercises, usually some time after the

This is a non-assessed exercise designed to give you the opportunity to become familiar with the fictitious organization around which the assessment centre exercises have been designed.

Information about this organization is contained in the attached brief entitled: 'As You Like It Leisure: The assessment centre scenario.'

You will work in pairs. Your task is to read the brief and then animate the 'As You Like It Leisure' organization and its past and current changes in a visual format that can be presented to the rest of the group within a five-minute timeframe.

(There then follows an outline - which is not provided here – of the company and the particular challenges and specific issues it is facing, especially in the marketing department.)

Figure 2.2   Example of an icebreaker

discussion has commenced. The purpose of this move is to provide a focus and context for the group before the actors arrive; once they are there the actors can be briefed to shake up the group by requesting to see, for example, plans, aims and objectives. The actors can also be briefed to squabble and bicker in order to find out how adept group members are at defusing the row and moving the discussion forward.

If you find yourself in this situation, do not make the mistake of treating the professional role players as an amusement, or sideshow. Their deliberate intrusion into the process has a serious purpose. They are there to enhance the quality and realism of the group discussion and to give the interaction more point and thrust so that the evidence it provides is thrown up in sharper relief than would otherwise be the case. Participants at assessment centres have been observed to snigger at actors when they squabble, or even to look at the assessors as if what is going on is unreal. Your interests will be better served by concentrating your efforts on trying to show how well you can cope with the 'real life' situation that the professional role players have created.

Even though you know the actors are arriving at a designated time, it is a common error not to be ready for them. The cardinal sin is to be crowded around the flipchart still thrashing out the details of what to do while the actors, having entered the room without being noticed, have to wait before their presence is acknowledged. Nothing is more certain to start you all off on the wrong foot – especially if the actors begin to behave like angry consumers or clients.

What preparation can you realistically do for group discussions?

It is most unlikely that you will be able to persuade friends, relatives or colleagues to join you in a mock discussion, and even if you did it would likely be counterproductive because for them there would be nothing at stake. The best course of action for you is to focus on specific skills and how and when you might be required to use them. The self-audits provided in Appendix 1 are intended to help you in this respect – look in particular at 'oral communication skills' and 'getting on with people'. For example, how well do you speak in front of others? Are you petrified, or can you cope? Be positive and think of times when you managed to do it successfully without hesitation or running out of relevant things to say.

What sort of team player are you? It is vital that you understand yourself in this respect. Many people imagine without thinking that they are good at working effectively with others as part of a team but the truth can be otherwise. For example, one of the authors of this book knows that he is not really a team player, but he also knows that he is not such an out-and-out individualist that he cannot work within a team as long as it is for a particular purpose and for a certain length of time.

Group exercises tend to attract a certain amount of fear and even loathing on the part of candidates. They are widely regarded as something to be got through, and not to be taken too seriously. You should forget all of that. Instead, try to be the one person who 'bucks the trend' and takes it seriously. When you see the group discussion exercise coming up on the programme get your head into gear and say to yourself that this is where you can really score well relative to the others. When Lance Armstrong won the Tour de France in 2000 he did it by slaughtering his rivals on a single mountain stage in the Pyrenees. And he did the same in 1999! In other words, when the going gets tough, the tough get going.

What assessors do not want to see

Assessors will view the following in a negative light:

- aberrant non-verbal behaviour such as sitting in such a way as to be apart from the rest, or turning your back on others, or looking petulant as if you would rather 'take your ball home' with you;
- talking over others, cutting across others and anything that might be construed as aggressive or even bullying;
- giving other people jobs to do such as scribing, chairing, timekeeping;
- poring over the paperwork constantly showing that you are not on top of the brief;
- ridiculing what someone else says;
- getting the 'wrong end of the stick' and wasting the group's time;

- keeping quiet while at the same time managing to look above it all;
- cracking dubious jokes.

Commit too many of these 'crimes' and it is likely that the assessors will draw the conclusion that you will not 'fit in' with future working groups. However, if you can avoid most of them, whilst being constructively engaged in the group's tasks, you will have a good chance of attracting a good evaluation from the assessors.

Chapter 3

How to succeed at making presentations

If you attend an assessment centre you can expect to be asked to give an oral presentation of some kind. It may take the form of an individual or a group presentation. The audience may be one or more assessors only or (more rarely) a mixture of assessors and other candidates.

Like others before you, you will probably find the prospect of giving a presentation daunting. Don't be alarmed – even experienced people can feel like that. Better to be keyed up with the adrenalin flowing than so laid back that you don't perform to the best of your ability. The fact is that presentation skills have never been more important. The aim of this chapter, therefore, is to provide you with guidance on: planning and preparing a presentation; delivering it effectively; and how your performance will be evaluated.

Planning and preparation

A good starting point would be to undertake an audit of your oral communication skills using the checklist provided in Appendix 1, if you have not already done so. If your self-evaluation is honest, you should learn something about the strengths on which you can build and the areas that you need to improve.

Thorough planning and preparation are essential for success with presentations, especially if you are relatively inexperienced. You really can prepare for these events – and get the payoff. If we had to provide just one tip it would be this – get the content right and the delivery will follow suit (but it won't take care of itself because you still have work to do). If you go into the presentation still unsure about whether you should say this or that, or how to start (will that joke backfire?), or whether you have too much material, then you are very likely to disintegrate before the audience's eyes. Strong content is the prerequisite for a strong performance.

So what should your preparation include? The first thing to do is to make certain that you follow closely any instructions you have been given. In this respect, you should pay particular attention to the following aspects of your brief:

- what you are expected to talk about (the subject matter of your presentation);
- the time you have been allocated;
- whether or not you are expected to invite or answer questions from your audience.

You should also be prepared for the possibility that your presentation will be video recorded so that your performance can be viewed later by the assessors as part of the assessment–selection process. If that turns out to be the case don't allow yourself to be 'thrown' – just try to carry on with your presentation as if the camera wasn't there. That should not be too difficult because the equipment will probably be in a fixed position and will simply blend into the furniture of the room.

Having established the basic parameters of the exercise you should then try to do what every presenter has to do:

● Find out what your audience is likely to know about the content of your presentation so that you can build upon that knowledge rather than repeating it. But don't make assumptions: they can be fatal.

● Acquire as thorough a knowledge of the content of your talk as you can without overloading your mind with needless information – try to separate the important from the unimportant.

● Make any visual aids (for the overhead projector, or IT package) you plan to use. If you are creating transparencies, make them clear and don't use the excuse 'sorry about the handwriting – normally I would use Powerpoint' because it doesn't cut any ice.

● Devise an outline plan for the session. You may find it helpful to make use of headings but whatever you do try to restrict yourself to one side of A4 or both sides of a card (see below) – there is nothing worse than having to scrabble among pieces of paper.

● Ensure, if possible (it won't always be), that the room in which the presentation is to be delivered is set out correctly for your purposes, and that all the equipment you require is present and that you know how to operate it (see the checklist given in Figure 3.1).

Structuring your presentation

In planning your presentation you should try to break it up into a number of sections, each of which should be given a sub-title or heading. For each section, list the key points you wish to make. You might find it helpful to:

● Write your headings and key points on a wallboard or flipchart in advance.
● Prepare some overhead transparencies or IT package graphics for the purpose. The advantage of doing this is that you will be able to show each one in turn at the appropriate point in your presentation – indeed they may help you to keep to the stated content of your presentation.
● Make yourself a set of brief notes on pieces of card (150 mm × 100 mm) – one card per section of your presentation. Card is much better than paper, but it will not necessarily be provided so take some with you to the assessment centre – it is allowed.

The big advantage of using visual aids is that they will be helpful to your audience in marking out your path, so facilitating concentration. Correct deployment should also ensure that you deal systematically with all the main points in your presentation. Some people manage without visual aids, but you have to be quite confident to sit down alongside the assessors and take them through your pitch.

Getting your presentation off to a good start

Try to give a clear and succinct introduction in which you:

- Introduce yourself, and if appropriate the organization (imaginary or real) you represent, for example: 'My name is… I am currently employed as a… in the marketing division of…' We say 'imaginary' because there might be a mild role-playing element built into the scenario, which you would need to address.
- Set out the main aims of your presentation. The old advice applies: 'tell them what you are going to tell them, tell them, tell them what you told them.'
- In that regard, indicate how you plan to structure your presentation ('I plan to deal first with the background to the plan, then to explain how that plan will be implemented and conclude by describing…')
- Tell the audience how you would prefer to deal with questions. If you are prepared to take them 'on the hoof', say so. As a token of confidence it will do you no harm in the eyes of the assessors (who usually like to interject anyway) but it can be a high-risk strategy in that you can lose your thread or worse unravel. If you would prefer to reserve questions until the end you can say something like: 'Finally, could I ask you to save your questions until the end of my presentation. However, if I use any technical terms or jargon that you don't understand, please feel free to ask me to explain what I mean.'
- Do not under any circumstances apologize for your lack of experience in making presentations. What allowances can the assessors possibly make?

Delivering your presentation

In delivering your presentation you should:

- Use 'marker' words and phrases such as 'the first point I want to make...', 'secondly...', and 'the most important aspect of company policy has been to...'; the aim here is to reinforce the structure of your presentation as set out in your introduction.
- Simplify the language used, for example:
  - use simple sentences to avoid confusing the listeners;
  - make sure that you define any technical or legal terms (jargon) and that they are understood by your audience.
- Try to exemplify and reinforce what you say by integrating examples into your presentation with which the audience is likely to be familiar. The aim here should be to:
  - avoid becoming 'bogged down' in detail so that the listeners have too much information to make sense of;
  - establish and consolidate the main points that you are trying to make.
- Remember to recapitulate or summarize what you have said at predetermined points such as the end of a section – for example, 'the main points, then, of company policy on recruitment and selection are...'; once again, the aim is to help the audience to 'keep track' of where you are in your presentation. If you can remember to do so, this is also a good way for you to check on your timing.

Keeping your eye on the audience

Make sure that you look at the audience while you are talking. Establish strong eye contact with them – all of them if there are several, especially those at the edges. That is where Bill Clinton is so good; if you watch him closely you will see that he always trains his gaze on the fringes of his audience so as to draw them in to his ambit. By doing this he is being inclusive, and that is important.

Of course, Clinton is blessed with autocue and you are not. If you do have to keep referring to your notes do not, on any account, bury your head in them. By keeping your head up you can help the audience to concentrate on what you are saying and pick up non-verbal clues from the body language of the audience about whether or not they are paying attention to, and are interested in, your presentation.

By monitoring audience reaction in that way, you can make some minor changes to what you are saying and how you say it, for example by moving on more quickly than you had intended to the next section or pausing to invite a question from the audience.

Your own body language

Eye contact (or lack of it) is just one form of non-verbal communication used by a speaker during a presentation. Indeed, tone and gesture can be more important than the actual words you use. It has been claimed that what you actually say counts as little as 7 per cent towards the overall impression you make. Whether it is 7 per cent or whatever, the point is good – does anyone ever take any notice of what Bill Clinton really says? Do not, however, draw the conclusion that content doesn't matter – it does. It is the effort you make with the 7 per cent (what you actually say) that helps you with the other 93 per cent.

You should try, therefore, to create an impression of self-confidence:

● Stand well – head easily upright and looking comfortably ahead, chest and shoulders held well, stomach under control and feet slightly apart. Remember that fidgeting with your hands, folding your arms rigidly across your chest (definitely to be avoided) and going on lengthy 'walkabouts' may communicate to the audience that you are nervous and even defensively 'uptight'. Even what might appear a neutral deployment of your arms, by folding them in a V in front of you with one hand over the other, is likely to come across as stiff. A good tip is to hold something in one hand. A card, if you are using one, is a very natural 'prop'. You can also use it to point at a flip sheet or at a transparency.

● Sit well – upper body as above, but leaning slightly forward. Avoid creating a bad impression by slouching 'casually' in the chair. This can happen when you forget where you are and crave the need to be informal so as to slacken the tension. Built into the presentation may be an element of role play that requires you to present to a senior person or board of directors, and slouching would be particularly inappropriate for this. Because you need to be able to see everybody's face you should only give your presentation from a sitting position when faced with a small audience (for example, less than 10).

● Use gestures (movements of the hands and arms) to underline what you are saying. However, avoid movements such as twitches and fidgets and hand chops and spreads, which are likely to distract the attention of the audience.

● Use facial expressions (smiles, grimaces and expressions of surprise) to reinforce what you are saying. Make them aware that you are alive and not a zombie. In that regard, avoid 'pre-cooked' jokes. The best humour will come from unrehearsed cracks or ripostes. Even old chestnuts will bring a smile to the assessors' faces and help release the tension. 'Are you ready to start?' 'As ready as I will ever be.'

Voice and speech

Try to speak conversationally by imagining that you are talking to people that you know well. You should also try to:

- Set the 'volume' at the right level at the outset by asking the audience (especially those at the back) if they can all hear you clearly.
- Speak clearly and distinctly.
- Vary the tone of your voice (quiet to loud) and the pace of your speech (slow to fast).
- Avoid using 'er' and 'um' – it is better to have a silent pause.

Using visual aids

You may be expected to make use of an overhead projector or an IT package as an aid to the delivery of your presentation. If you have had little or no experience of using equipment of this kind you would be well advised to practise in advance. Take time – ask for time – to become acquainted with the switch that turns on the projector, to adjust the screen. How many times have candidates become flustered right at the start because they can't turn the machine on? Taking these precautionary steps will increase the competence with which you use the equipment and your confidence. It will also leave you free to concentrate on other things like what you are saying and how you are saying it. Figure 3.1 offers a checklist of things to do and things not to do when using visual aids.

Concluding your presentation

Try to bring your presentation to a telling conclusion by:

- Letting the audience know that the end is in sight.

- Summarizing the main points you made in your presentation.
- Thanking them for their attention.

What to do when using visual aids

✓ Make your projected visual images clear and simple.

✓ Make sure that people in all parts of the room (especially the back) can read them clearly.

✓ Use bullet points rather than large passages of text.

✓ Make sure that their content is consistent with what you are saying.

✓ Make sure they are in the correct sequence (one that conforms to your plan).

✓ Try to be economical in the number you use – too many diminishes their impact, leads to boredom and can cause you to run out of time.

What not to do when using visual aids

✗ Don't stand in a position that obstructs the audience's view, for example in front of the overhead projector screen.

✗ Don't talk to the screen instead of the audience – watch how the best TV weather presenters do it.

✗ Don't simply repeat what the audience can read on the screen – it is intended as an aid to what you say not a substitute.

Figure 3.1 What to do and what not to do when using visual aids

- Inviting them to ask questions (if that is part of your brief or part of a 'contract' you made with the audience at the start of your presentation).

Having asked the audience to keep their questions until the end, do not accept them in mid-talk unless you want to. As we said before, assessors are often keen to interject – they don't just want to talk for the sake of talking, they do it with a purpose in mind. If you get a question that you find difficult to answer you may find it helpful to:

- Say that you cannot answer it at that moment but that you will think about it and discuss it with the questioner afterwards.
- Give a tentative or partial answer (in other words, your best current answer) and ask members of the audience if they can better it.
- Ask a counterquestion – ask the questioner to explain what lies behind the question, or to give her/his opinion on the issue raised. But don't be too cute; this ploy can backfire when an assessor, seeing what you are doing, insists that you answer the question as stated.
- Refer questioners to material such as the case study documents in which they can find the answer.

There is nothing wrong with going beyond the question and throwing in some other thoughts, and you may get credit – but don't overdo it.

What will the assessors be looking for?

The assessors will be looking at, and listening to, your presentation and in so doing will form an overall evaluation of your

performance. They will use a set of assessment c
apply a rating scale to each criterion. The precise term
these criteria may vary but in general they will all be looking
closely at:

- how well you have planned and prepared your presentation including its content, structure and visual aids;
- the confidence with which you delivered your presentation;
- your oral communication skills, including your style of speaking;
- your skills in using the flipchart, overhead projector, or IT package;
- how well you answered questions (how well you thought on your feet);
- how well you handled the pressure of the occasion.

Summary

Some detailed guidance has been provided above on how to succeed in giving presentations. That advice can be summarized as follows:

- Thorough preparation is essential and it will reward you – never do a presentation 'off the cuff'.
- Start with a clear introduction in which you tell the audience what you plan to talk about.
- Give your presentation a clear structure and communicate that to the audience.
- Make a list of key points you intend to make in each section of your address.
- Use marker phrases such as 'the first point I want to

make...', and 'the most important thing to remember is...' to focus the attention of the audience on what you are saying.

- Use examples to reinforce and consolidate the points you are making.
- At intervals during your presentation recap on what you have said.
- Use simple sentences to avoid confusing the listeners.
- Explain any terms ('jargon') you use with which your audience might be unfamiliar.
- Take time at the outset to familiarize yourself with the technology.
- Make and maintain eye contact with members of the audience when you are talking to them.
- Carry yourself well throughout.
- Avoid distracting gestures and movements.
- Avoid being overly informal as a way of dealing with the strain.
- Conclude by reminding the listeners of the main points that you have made and inviting questions.

Finally, at the very end, do not grab your papers and bolt – you will only give the impression that you're glad that the ordeal is over and that you can't wait to get away.

Chapter 4

How to succeed in selection tests

The aim of this chapter is to develop your knowledge and understanding of selection tests by providing you with:

- a brief guide to different types of test;
- opportunities to work through examples of some of the most commonly used tests;
- suggestions on how to prepare for, and succeed in, such tests.

Sources of practice tests are listed on page 138.

What are tests and why do employers use them?

Put simply, tests are designed to measure how good people are at doing certain things – often as a basis for predicting their future performance. Those that are designed to measure intellectual capability are called 'ability tests', 'cognitive tests', or 'psychometric tests'. Those used at assessment centres to choose people for jobs or further training are known as 'selection tests'. Such tests seek to establish the aptitudes that the applicants have (or do not have) for certain kinds of work and/or particular jobs.

The tests used at an assessment centre may also include 'personality tests' (sometimes known as 'inventories' or 'questionnaires') that are designed to measure those aspects of your personality that employers consider to be significant. It might be important, for example, for them to know if you are the kind of person who can stay calm but alert in the conditions that prevail in the workplace. Personality tests help them to choose the people they think are best suited to the job.

Tests usually involve a pencil and paper, although increasingly they are computer based. In order to ensure the fairness, consistency and reliability of the results such tests should be:

● taken under standardized conditions including strict adherence to time limits;
● administered by someone who has been trained in their use and has been certified as competent – in the UK this is done by the British Psychological Society (BPS);
● objectively marked, for example with the use of an electronic scanning machine.

All of the selection tests used by employers will have been put through rigorous piloting trials before being put into practice. When you take a test you will find that they come complete with carefully worded instructions and examples that tell you what you have to do to tackle them correctly. So, you need to make a habit of reading test instructions carefully and working through the examples on all occasions, even when you think you are familiar with them already. You will find that in real tests you are usually allowed time to do this before the test begins – do not waste it!

Different types of test used at assessment centres

Employers make use of a wide range of tests when selecting candidates. The notes given below are intended to show what skills are being tested by different types of test. If you achieve a high score on a particular type of test it may indicate that you will do well in a job that requires you to apply the skill being tested. On the other hand, if you find that you do badly on a particular test it may be that you would have some difficulty in coping at this stage with jobs requiring proficiency in the skill being tested. Further work on your part to develop that skill might enable you to tackle the test more successfully at a later date.

Logical reasoning tests are used to measure a person's ability to solve problems by thinking logically on the basis of the information provided. These can sometimes take the form of abstract problems, or they can be similar to problems encountered in the work for which people are being selected. The ability to do well in this kind of test may tell you and a potential employer that you have the ability to think critically and to solve the problems that arise at work, such as deploying resources and forward planning.

Numerical reasoning tests are used to measure the ability to work accurately with numbers and to solve problems based on data presented in various forms such as diagrams, graphs and statistical tables. The ability to do well in this type of test is relevant to jobs that require you to work with money, interpret sales or production figures, or cope with the numerical aspects of science and technology.

Verbal reasoning tests are used to measure the ability to use language and comprehend the written word. At work this ability is relevant to tasks involving reading and writing instructions, letters and reports. At a simple level they may set out to test your basic literacy, including your ability to write grammatically correct sentences and to spell and punctuate correctly. Missing word tests, examples of which are given below, fall into this category. At a more advanced level verbal reasoning tests are looking for the ability of the candidates to understand the meaning of what has been written or said. This capacity to make sense from text is tested in the hidden sentences and sentence sequences tests.

Technical tests are used to measure skills and abilities that are relevant to various kinds of employment. Typically, these include questions that assess the ability to understand technical ideas expressed in a mathematical form (including diagrams) and to understand how mechanical things work.

Similarly, *clerical tests*, which require candidates to check and classify data under time pressure, are used to measure their clerical skills.

The worked examples and sample questions given below are taken from some of the types of test most commonly used at assessment centres. If you work your way through them it should give you a good idea of what is involved in each case. **The answers to the sample questions are given at the end of the chapter.** Working through the sample questions should also help you to begin to identify where your strengths and weaknesses might lie when it comes to taking real tests. Whether or not that is the case, you would be well advised to develop your skills further by means of practice tests (see page 138).

Examples from a logical reasoning test

With the two sample questions given below your task is to work out which is the correct answer in each case, using the information provided. You should:

- study the data very carefully before you attempt to answer the questions;
- record your answer by putting a tick alongside the option(s) you have chosen;
- use scrap paper for any rough work you need to do;
- allow yourself about *five minutes* to solve each problem – this will help to give you an idea of the time pressure you would have to work under in a real test.

Q1

Imagine that you work for a company that offers coach tours of London to visiting tourists. Each coach tour has a courier who gives a commentary for the tourists for the duration of the trip. Most of the tourists are from overseas, so all of your couriers can speak at least two foreign languages as follows: Phil can speak French, German, Italian and Russian; Sue can speak Russian, French and Japanese; Duleep can speak Spanish and Greek; Trish can speak French, German, Italian and Greek; Wavell can speak French and Spanish; Amanda can speak Italian and Greek. On a particular day, you must organize six coach trips for a party of Japanese, a party of Russians, a party of Spanish, a party of French, a party of Germans and a party of Italians. All of the coach tours are scheduled to take place simultaneously. *Who will be the courier for the French party?*

A = Phil	B = Sue	C = Duleep
D = Trish	E = Wavell	F = Amanda

Q2

You are a club secretary who has the job of making the arrangements for a day excursion. The members have been given the details of five possibilities, called A, B, C, D and E, and have been asked to place them in their order of preference. When the results were analysed it was found that they could be arranged into eight groups. The table below shows the order of preference of each of the eight groups of club members. It is not possible to arrange all five excursions, but the committee has decided that it will be possible to arrange two. As club secretary you have been told to choose the two that will allow every member to have either their first or their second choice. *Which two excursions will you choose?*

| | A | B | C | D | E |

Group of members	Excursions in order of preference				
1	E	D	B	C	A
2	B	A	C	E	D
3	A	B	E	C	D
4	C	B	A	E	D
5	D	E	C	A	B
6	A	B	D	C	E
7	A	D	B	E	C
8	D	C	A	B	E

Examples from numerical reasoning tests

Number problems

The examples given below are from a multiple-choice test in

which you are presented with a fairly simple problem and are required to select the correct answer from five possible answers. Number problem tests of this kind are based on the four basic arithmetical operations (addition, subtraction, division and multiplication), simple fractions, decimals and percentages applied to quantities of money, objects, speed, time and area. You are *not* allowed to use a calculator. However, you are permitted to use a sheet of paper or a note pad for any rough work. The sample questions given below should help you to get an idea of what is involved. In each case, record your answer by putting a tick alongside the option you have chosen.

Q3
How much money would it cost to buy seven loaves of bread at 52p a loaf?

A = £3.44	B = £3.54	C = £3.64
D = £3.74	E = £3.84	

Q4
If I pay £4.56 for a tin of paint and 85p for a brush, how much will I have spent in total?

A = £5.31	B = £5.41	C = £5.51
D = £5.61	E = £5.71	

Q5
Two out of every eight cyclists are questioned in a spot check. Out of 408 cyclists, how many are questioned?

A = 102	B = 100	C = 88
D = 80	E = 40	

Q6

A worker's shift begins at 05.30 and lasts for nine hours. What time does it end?

A = 15.30   B = 15.00   C = 14.30

D = 14.00   E = 13.30

Q7

If my bus journey takes 35 minutes and my train journey takes 55 minutes, how long is my journey in total?

A = 1½ hours   B = 1¼ hours   C = 70 minutes

D = ¾ hour   E = 85 minutes

Data interpretation

This is another multiple-choice test that is commonly used in personnel selection. In this test you are given a series of statistical tables, graphs or diagrams followed by questions related to each data set. For each question there are five possible answers, A to E. Your task is to work out which is the correct answer to each question, using the data provided and without the use of a calculator. Now work your way through the sample questions provided below, recording your answer in each case by putting a tick alongside the option you have chosen.

Q8

The following table shows the price of fuel for heating in pence per useful kilowatt hour:

Fuel	Pence
Butane (room heater)	4.6
Electricity (fan heater)	5.2
Kerosene (central heating)	2.9
Gas (wall heater)	1.7
Coal (open fire)	3.5
Anthracite (central heating)	2.2

Which heating fuel is approximately twice the price of gas?

A = Butane   B = Electricity   C = Kerosene
D = Coal   E = Anthracite

Q9

The following table shows the number of emergencies attended by six Fire Brigade sub-stations during a five-month period:

Sub-station	May	June	July	Aug	Sept
A	11	10	12	26	27
B	22	23	20	42	28
C	36	46	58	68	43
D	21	22	24	27	26
E	16	16	15	19	12
F	24	18	26	37	29

What was the total number of emergencies attended by all six sub-stations in June and July?

A = 283   B = 309   C = 290
D = 310   E = 287

Number sequences

The worked examples and the sample questions given below are similar to those used in number sequence tests, which are commonly used in personnel selection. You will find that in this type of test, each question is presented in the form of a line that contains a sequence of numbers, but one number is missing and has been replaced with an 'xx'. In all cases the answer is a two-digit number. Your task is to work out that missing number. Given below are three worked examples to give you an idea of what is involved. When you have studied them, try to do the sample questions that follow. Record your answers in the spaces provided.

Examples

1.	3	7	11	xx	19	Answer = 15
2.	1	2	4	8	xx	Answer = 16
3.	6 1 7	12 3 15		2 10 xx		Answer = 12

In *Example 1*, the numbers increase by four:

$$3 (+ 4) = 7 (+ 4) = 11 (+ 4) = 15 (+ 4) = 19.$$

The missing number (or xx), therefore, is 15.

In *Example 2*, the numbers increase by a factor of 2 as follows:

$$1 (\times 2) = 2 (\times 2) = 4 (\times 2) = 8 (\times 2) = 16.$$

The missing number (or xx), therefore, is 16.

In *Example 3*, the numbers are in groups of three and, in each group of three, the second number added to the first equals the third. So:

$$6 + 1 = 7; 12 + 3 = 15; 2 + 10 = 12.$$

The missing number (or xx), therefore, is 12.

Q10	3	10	xx	24	31			xx = ...
Q11	24	19	15	xx	10			xx = ...
Q12	2	4	12	xx	240			xx = ...
Q13	7	15	23	26	23	xx	7	xx = ...
Q14	3	5	9	17	xx			xx = ...

Examples from verbal reasoning tests

Missing words

In this type of verbal reasoning test you will find sentences in which two gaps have been left. As a candidate, your task is to decide what those missing words are. Below each sentence you will find four pairs of words, with a letter (A, B, C and D) above each pair. You have to work out which *one* pair of words fits into the spaces correctly. Sometimes it is a question of the spelling of the words or their meaning. At other times it is a matter of the correct use of grammar. In some of the items the right answer will be 'none of these', in which case you would record your decision by writing the letter E in the answer space provided. The sample questions given below should help you to get the idea.

Q15
Three senior managers _____ present at the _____

A	B	C	D
was	was	were	were
enquirey	enquiry	enquiry	enquirey

E None of these   Answer = ...

Q16

A witness was _____ talking to the _____

A	B	C	D
scene	seen	scene	scene
suspect	susspect	susspect	suspect

E None of these   Answer = ...

Mixed sentences

In verbal reasoning tests of this type you are given a series of sentences in which the positions of *two* words have been interchanged so that the sentences no longer make sense. You have to read each sentence carefully and pick out the two words, then underline them in pencil. The example given below should help you to understand what you have to do. When you have studied it, try the sample questions provided.

Example: Some planning developments permit householders to carry out whatever authorities they wish.

Answer: The sentence should read: Some planning authorities permit householders to carry out whatever developments they wish. So to record your answer the two words you would underline in the sentence are: 'developments' and 'authorities'.

Q17

Even when exhausted and afloat, a person will remain unconscious until he can be rescued, provided he is wearing a life jacket.

Q18
The snow on the greatest summits of the Alps, the lakes with their deep blue water and the woods full of flowers are among some of the highest beauties of nature.

Q19
We shall have cold salad at 9 o'clock; there will be cold meat, supper, sandwiches, fruit, sweets and trifle.

Q20
Too much rain ruins the crops, if they are also poor but it does not rain at all.

Q21
Before children start school in Great Britain at five years they must be six while going to school in Italy.

Word links

In this type of verbal reasoning test your task is to identify two words in the *lower line, one in each half,* that form a 'verbal analogy' when paired with the words in the upper line. Put simply, a verbal analogy is an agreement or similarity in the meaning of words. The two examples given below will give an idea of what you have to do in this type of test. When you have worked your way through them try to do the sample questions provided.

Example 1

FISH   WATER

fin   bird   trout   sand   air   sea

In this case 'bird' and 'air' are the correct answers because birds are found in the air in the same way as fish are found in water. With this type of analogy the general rule is: 'the top left word is to the top right word as a bottom left word is to a bottom right word.'

Example 2

HANGAR   GARAGE

field   engineer   plane   mechanic   car   house

Here plane and car are the correct answers because a plane is kept in a hangar just as a car is kept in a garage. With this type of analogy the general rule is: 'the top left word is to a bottom left word as the top right word is to a bottom right word.' When tackling the sample questions given below you should: note that the correct answers will always conform to one of the two general rules identified above – you will have to work out for yourself which one is used in each question; record your answer in each question by underlining the two words you have chosen in pencil.

Q22

COURT   LAW

church   service   vicar   hymns   religion   tennis

Q23

BOOK   READER

paper   text   radio   listener   news   signal

Q24

FLOWERS   VASE

paint   mural   picture   canvas   frame   compost

Q25

FLOOR   CARPET

mattress   settee   rig   sheet   pullover   pillowcase

Q26

PEOPLE   LIBRARY

cow   book   individual   dairy   diary   book

Hidden sentences

In this type of verbal reasoning test each question consists of a single sentence, to which a number of irrelevant words have been added. These words are scattered throughout the sentence in order to make it 'hidden'. Your task is to find that hidden sentence. So, you have to read through each question carefully in order to decide what the sentence should be. Then you have to indicate the *first three words* and the *last three words* of the sentence by underlining them in pencil. To help you check that you have identified it correctly, the number of words in the original sentence is given in brackets at the end of the item – for example [12]. It is necessary to count the words very carefully to ensure that you do not make a mistake. A sentence is only acceptable if it contains exactly the number of words indicated in the brackets. Where hyphens occur (for example, five-year...), count two words. The following example should help you to understand what you have to do. When you have studied it work your way through the sample questions provided.

Example
with because the advent of new television ratings created a exciting revolution in leisure days patterns of hobbies   [10]

Answer
The original sentence was: 'The advent of television created a revolution in leisure patterns.'

In the test, therefore, you should mark your answer like this:

with because <u>the advent of</u> new television ratings created a exciting revolution <u>in leisure</u> days <u>patterns</u> of hobbies   [10]

In other words, you should underline the *first three words* in the sentence ('the', 'advent' and 'of') and the *last three words* in the sentence ('in', 'leisure' and 'patterns').

Q27
keep out this polythene around in out of length reach of also and children if to not avoid the baby having danger of the suffocation   [14]

Q28
when they this product is obsolete using manufactured by after from 100% recycled paper writing and will uses some no wood pulp fiction   [13]

Q29
in fact we make up blurs with stories fiction when in this documentary focusing about two a cameraman who comes from search   [10]

Q30

at one the of talk I found out why it difficult how to understand concentration and some so lost gave interest sharing together

[10]

Q31

making an studies game of fun while children playing up suggest games that in themselves there are too three causes also enjoyment of conflict [12]

Sentence sequences

In this type of verbal reasoning test you are given a series of prose passages, each consisting of four sentences. In each case the original order of the sentences has been changed. In other words, they are now out of sequence. Your task is to read each passage and work out what the correct sequence should be. In tests of this type you should:

● begin by reading through the sentences in each question to get the sense of the passage;
● then work out the correct sequence of the sentences – the order in which they were originally written;
● use the numbers (1 to 4) given in brackets at the front of the sentences to record the correct sequence in the spaces provided.

The following example should help you to understand what to do. When you have studied it try to answer the sample questions given below.

Example: (1) There you will be issued with the key to your bedroom and your training folder. (2) This will normally be in the same building as the reception and your bedroom. (3) Upon arrival at the training centre please book in at reception. (4) The folder will contain a list of the training rooms and, having deposited your luggage in your room, you should go to the first training room listed.

Answer: To make sense the passage should read as follows:

(3) Upon arrival at the training centre please book in at reception. (1) There you will be issued with the key to your bedroom and your training folder. (4) The folder will contain a list of the training rooms and, having deposited your luggage in your room, you should go to the first training room listed. (2) This will normally be in the same building as the reception and your bedroom.

The correct *sequence*, therefore, is: 3, 1, 4 and 2, which should be recorded in the answer spaces as follows:

Answer   1 = 3   2 = 1   3 = 4   4 = 2

Q32
(1) It is, however, the longest way and if you do not need to go there I would suggest that you go the other way. (2) One route would take you down past the Post Office. (3) I would advise you to take that one if you need to conduct any business there. (4) There are two ways in which you can get to the supermarket from here.

Answer   1 = ... 2 = ... 3 = ... 4 = ...

Q33
(1) Confidential records will then be kept but no names or addresses will be recorded on them, only a number that the staff will allocate to users of the service. (2) Yes, totally. (3) At

first, a verbal contract will be made between the client and staff member. (4) Is the service confidential?

Answer   1 = ...   2 = ...   3 = ...   4 = ...

Q34
(1) The Commission's chairperson, in presenting the report, commented that wider and more effective anti-discrimination legislation was necessary. (2) The demands came as the Commission presented its annual report, which records evidence of widespread discrimination. (3) Demands for a tough new racial discrimination law were made today, amid warnings of an end to the fragile peace in Britain's inner cities. (4) Specifically, the Commission for Racial Equality wants measures to prevent racial discrimination to be extended to central and local government.

Answer   1 = ...   2 = ...   3 = ...   4 = ...

Comprehension/critical thinking

This is a multiple-choice test in which you are given several prose passages, each of which is followed by a set of questions or incomplete statements related to its content. After reading a passage your task is to choose, from the alternatives given, the best answer or answers to each question, or the best ending to the statement. In each case you are told the number, one or two, of answers required. In the sample item given below you will find an extract of text that is followed by two questions (A and B), each of which in turn offers you five choices (1–5). Your task is to read the text and then answer the questions by putting ticks alongside what you consider to be the correct choices.

Q35

For almost 30 years, after it first captured nearly half of the global market, Japan dominated world shipbuilding. Even during the decade when the decline in the shipbuilding industry in other countries had been exacerbated by the entry of South Korea into the international market, Japan managed to hold on to its position. However, the cost it had to pay for this was high. Japan's shipbuilding companies had to lower their capacity by over one third and to reduce their work force by almost as much as their counterparts in the UK. This created particular difficulties for Japan's big shipbuilders, because of their commitment to providing their employees with employment for life. Although some of the workforce who were surplus to requirements could be redeployed in new industries and many others could be retired, it was difficult to cater for them all by these means and the guarantee of employment for life, so crucial in the industrial life of Japan, was put at risk.

A   The decline in Japan's shipbuilding industry has (2 answers)

1   been equal to that in the UK
2   occurred despite the increase in its share of the world market
3   resulted in a lowering of the costs of production
4   had high economic and social costs
5   threatened industrial relations in the country

B   The world decline in shipbuilding was (1 answer)

1   caused by Japan sustaining its output levels
2   a result of Japan's policy of employment for life
3   caused by vigorous marketing by the South Koreans

4   caused by a general decline in the demand for new vessels
5   the result of Japan's continued dominance of world
     markets

How important is it to do well on selection tests?

Increasingly, a good performance on tests such as those described above is important in securing employment, or access to further training. It may determine, for example, whether or not you proceed to later stages in the selection process at an assessment centre (see the sample timetable given in Figure 1.1). However, it is important to put tests into perspective. Before they offer you a job most organizations will take into consideration the other information they have about you in your 'profile' as well as your tests scores. Consequently, a modest performance on a test may be offset by some or all of the following:

● the strength of your formal qualifications;
● your previous work and life experience;
● the way you perform in an interview;
● how well you cope with the other work-related exercises set for you at the assessment centre.

Conversely, an outstanding test score may not be sufficient to compensate for serious weaknesses detected elsewhere at the assessment centre.

Can practice make a difference?

Experience suggests that many candidates underachieve in selection tests because they are over-anxious, and because they have not known what to expect. Practice tests, which are available via publishers such as Kogan Page (see page 138), are designed to help you to overcome both of these common causes of failure. Regular practice will also give you the opportunity to work under conditions similar to those you will experience when taking real tests. In particular, you should become accustomed to working under the pressure of the strict time limits imposed in real test situations. Familiarity with the demands of the tests and working under simulated test conditions should help you to cope better with any nervousness you experience when taking tests that really matter. Strictly speaking, the old adage that 'practice makes perfect' may not apply to selection tests but it can make a difference.

It has been impossible in the space available in this book to give you more than an introduction to some of the main types of psychometric tests that you might encounter at an assessment centre and to provide you with a small number of sample questions for you to try out for yourself. If, when you have done this, you decide that you need more practice you would be well advised to consult some of the other books in the Kogan Page series (see page 138). Many of these tests have been specially written for the purpose of providing practice tests designed to help you develop your ability to cope with cognitive tests of different types.

How to perform to the best of your ability on tests

Our experience suggests that if you want to perform to the best of your ability on psychometric tests used for selection purposes you would be well advised to follow the advice given below:

- Make sure that you know what you have to do before you start – if you do not understand ask the supervisor.
- Read the instructions carefully before the test starts in order to make sure that you understand them.
- Skim reading through this part of the test is not good enough – it can cause you to overlook important details and to make mistakes that are easily avoidable.
- Even if you have taken a test before do not assume that the instructions (and the worked examples) are the same as last time – they might have been changed. Read them as carefully as you can.
- If it helps, highlight or underline the 'command words' in the instructions – those words that tell you what you have to do.
- Once the test begins, work as quickly and accurately as you can. Remember, every unanswered question is a scoring opportunity missed!
- Check frequently to make sure that the question you are answering matches the space you are filling in on the answer grid.
- Avoid spending too much time on questions you find difficult – leave them and go back later if you have time.
- If you are uncertain about an answer, enter your best reasoned choice (but try to avoid simply 'guessing').

- If you have some spare time after you have answered all the questions go back and check through your answers.
- Keep working as hard as you can throughout the test – the more correct answers you give the higher your score will be.
- Concentrate your mind on the test itself and nothing else – you cannot afford to allow yourself to be distracted.
- Be positive in your attitude – don't allow previous failures in tests and examinations to have a detrimental effect on your performance on this occasion. In other words, don't allow yourself to be 'beaten before you begin'!

You can begin to put this advice into effect by using the practice tests available via the sources listed on page 138. Used systematically, these should help you to establish good habits that will serve you well when you come to take real tests at an assessment centre.

Tests of personality and personality inventories

Personality tests or inventories are used at assessment centres to measure characteristics or traits that might affect an individual's performance at work. Your personality, as projected through your responses to tests or inventories, will be seen, therefore, as an important indicator of how well you are suited to the job on offer. Some of the tests that you may be required to take will have been designed to measure the strength of your vocational career interests.

The most commonly used tests involve responding to a series of questions, the answers to which are used to generate a profile of the candidate's personality. So, when you complete an inventory of this kind your answers will be used to show how you score on each personality trait. This will enable the assessors to compare your profile with those of the other candidates in order to see which of you appears to be best suited for the job. The personality characteristics used in such inventories include emotional stability, warmth, self-reliance, dominance, sensitivity and tension. The precise way in which your personal profile will be created will depend upon the particular test being used. However, most of them will seek to establish your score for each of the personality traits included in the inventory, as shown in the example given in Figue 4.1. The chances are that, with an inventory of this kind, your completed profile will include scores from both the left-hand and the right-hand sides of the scale – as do most candidates' profiles.

Factor	Left Meaning	Standard Ten Score 1 2 3 4 5 6 7 8 9 10	Right Meaning
Warmth	More emotionally distant from people	x x x x x x x x x x x	Attentive and warm to others
Emotional Stability	Reactive, emotionally changeable	x x x x x x x x x x x	Emotionally stable, adaptive

Figure 4.1 An example from a personality profile

The questions in personality tests differ from those used in ability tests in that there are no right and wrong answers. The simplest type of inventory asks questions that require 'yes' or 'no' answers. Others will ask you to put a tick against the statements that are most like you and a cross against those that are least like you. Another common approach is to ask you to rate yourself on a scale from 1 (strongly disagree) to 5 (strongly agree) on a number of statements. The number of items in a personality inventory of this kind can vary, but it is common to find 100 to 120. That number is needed to get a reliable 'fix' on several personality traits. A test of that length should normally take you about 30 to 40 minutes to complete.

As with the results of the ability tests, the outcome of your personality test will be considered alongside evidence of your performance on the whole range of exercises undertaken at the assessment centre. Having said that, it is unlikely (and in fact not desirable) that the results of the personality test alone will determine your fate. By the time the assessors make their final selection, therefore, they will have had ample opportunity to observe your behaviour at first hand. Hence, it would be unwise in these circumstances to answer the questions in the personality test in a way that you think is desired or expected. It is not in your interest to pretend that you are something you are not. So to do well – to be authentic – when completing a personality test:

● know yourself;
● respond honestly;
● be positive about yourself;
● remember that there are many different job roles and that these can be fulfilled successfully by people with different personal characteristics.

Taking ability and personality tests online

You may be asked to complete ability tests and/or personality inventories online. This could happen during the assessment centre or you could be asked to attend a location beforehand to complete the necessary test(s). There is nothing to worry about in doing electronic versions of tests – many people even find it to be more fun than completing paper-and-pencil tests. Given the medium in which we are writing it has been impossible to give you examples here, but why not go to the Web to complete a practice test or two? Here are some places to look:

- ASE Personality Test 16PF5 and others – www.ase-solutions.co.uk
- Morrisby Organisation Tests including an emotional intelligence test – www.morrisby.co.uk
- Saville & Holdsworth provide examples taken from verbal, numerical and diagrammatic reasoning tests – www.shldirect.com
- Tests from Team Technology – www.teamtechnology.co.uk

If you aspire to join the Civil Service, and especially the fast stream, you might find yourself being invited to attend a Civil Service assessment centre. In that eventuality you will no doubt want to practise the Civil Service Fast Stream Qualifying Test. There are two tests: data interpretation (numerical reasoning) and verbal organization (verbal reasoning), and each will take 20 to 30 minutes to complete. You can do these practice tests online by going to the following Web site: www.selfasses.faststream.gov.uk

Answers to sample questions

Logical reasoning

Q1 E (Wavell)
Q2 B and D

Number problems

Q3 C
Q4 B
Q5 A
Q6 C
Q7 A

Data interpretation

Q8 D (= Coal)
Q9 C (= 290)

Number sequences

Q10 xx = 17
Q11 xx = 12
Q12 xx = 48
Q13 xx = 15
Q14 xx = 33

Missing words

Q15 C
Q16 E

Mixed sentences

Q17 afloat; unconscious

Q18   greatest; highest
Q19   salad; supper
Q20   if; but
Q21   before; while

Word links

(Left-hand word first, right-hand word second.)

Q22   church; religion
Q23   radio; listener
Q24   picture; frame
Q25   mattress; sheet
Q26   individual; book

Hidden sentences

(First three words first, last three words second)

Q27   keep, this, polythene; danger, of, suffocation
Q28   this, product, is; no, wood, pulp
Q29   fact, blurs, with; about, a, cameraman
Q30   I, found, it; so, lost, interest
Q31   studies, of, children; causes, of, conflict

Sentence sequences

Q32   1 = 4;   2 = 2;   3 = 3;   4 = 1
Q33   1 = 4;   2 = 2;   3 = 3;   4 = 1
Q34   1 = 3;   2 = 4;   3 = 2;   4 = 1

Comprehension/critical thinking

Q35   A = 2 and 4;   B = 4

Chapter 5

How to succeed at panel interviews

The aim of this chapter is to explain why interviews are so popular with employers; how a panel interview differs from a one-to-one interview; how to prepare for a panel interview; and how to cope effectively once an interview starts. The general assumption is that you are applying for a job from outside the organization and that the interview will be part of the programme at an assessment centre. However, the advice is equally applicable if you are being considered for a job, or further training, within your current organization.

Why interviews are used so much

Interviews are popular because they give the employer the security of having seen candidates such as you in the flesh. It also gives you the opportunity to put your case to the organization, and to make some judgements about whether you want to work there or not. More fundamentally, people have come to expect an interview, and would be disappointed if they didn't get one. That is just as true for internal candidates as it is for external ones. People applying for jobs or promotion seem to have a deep-seated conviction that if they can just get in to see the interviewers they can tell their whole story. It is not quite the same at an assessment centre, where the interview is but one element of the whole event, but the rationale is no different.

Never forget that interviews are a two-way process. Employers should be trying to sell themselves to you almost as much as you are trying to sell yourself to them. The last thing they want is for you to reject them because you formed a negative impression of their organization during the interview. Indeed, you may well have formed such an impression from the assessment centre as a whole, but the interview is where you will sense it most strongly. The interview always serves a public-relations function.

How panel interviews differ from one-to-one interviews

The whole point of an assessment centre is to make a better job of assessing candidates than is the case with the one-to-one interview on which employers have relied for so long. If the one-to-one interview is the 'horse and cart' of personnel selection, then the assessment centre is the 'Rolls Royce'. Not only do your chances cease to depend on a single encounter, but for the interview element you are given a panel of interviewers.

Involving more interviewers in the selection process is obviously intended to produce fairer and more accurate choices. On the face of it the logic is fine. If it is true that many employers make up their mind about a potential candidate within three to five seconds of meeting her or him, the downside of relying on one interviewer to make the decision is clear. Nobody would want a jury to consist of one person. But panels, like juries, can be swayed, and if individual members share the same attitudes, opinions and biases their decisions are likely to converge very quickly. So a panel interview will be fairer than in a one-to-one interview more often than not, but panel interviews may not always deliver fairness.

Number of interviewers

The most offputting aspect of a panel interview is the number of people on the panel. Three should present no problems, but any number greater than that starts to become bothersome, especially if some are seated at the edges of your vision. In these circumstances it is easy to feel exposed and vulnerable, even intimidated. Unfortunately, that is how some employers, hopefully a minority, may want you to feel when they interview you. One of the authors remembers being given a seat at an interview facing the window so he had to screw up his eyes to see whenever the sun came out. Then there was the finance house that sat the candidate in a revolving chair placed in the centre of the room. Every time someone new asked a question the chair was spun so that the candidate was facing that questioner.

What is being described here is a 'school' of interviewing that thinks that if candidates can deal with gratuitous pressure in the interview they will be able to deal with pressure in the job. Thankfully, you should not have to face any of this at an assessment centre. If employers have gone to the trouble and expense of organizing and running an assessment centre it is most unlikely that they will engage in, or sanction the use of, any bullying tactics.

As far as panel numbers are concerned, don't let that worry you. Think of it this way. The more interviewers there are, the better your chances. You have got as far as the interview stage, you have your story to tell, and now you have your chance to do so. If one of the panel doesn't like what you have to say or how you say it all is not lost – there are others present and they may well think differently, even to the extent of seeking to influence those who have doubts about you. In any case, the panels you are likely to encounter at assessment centres will probably be on the small side because the number of assessors who can be assigned to any one activity is limited. Indeed, you may only have to face two interviewers, one of whom takes notes and hardly asks any questions.

Note taking

In a panel interview you will see more note taking than you are accustomed to seeing in a one-to-one interview where the interviewer is usually too hard-pressed to scribble much down. Obviously in a panel situation there are always people free to take notes. In fact, someone may well have been delegated the job of taking notes on behalf of the panel but that will not stop others taking notes if they want to do so.

Note taking is something you have to get used to. Regard it as part and parcel of the interview – like asking questions or the invitation to you to ask questions. Forget about how much or how little note taking is going on, or whether a burst of activity on the part of the panel members is related to anything you just said. Unless there is someone there taking verbatim notes, and you will quickly realize who this is, the amount and frequency of note taking is not driven in any direct way by anything you are doing. Interviewers are obliged to take notes, increasingly for legal reasons – for example, in the case of a disputed decision they might have to be produced at an industrial tribunal. However, the main reason is to avoid relying on their memories when it comes to collating evidence about you and the other candidates. As the saying goes: 'better a short pencil than a long memory.'

Observers

Panels can contain observers as well as active interviewers. If there are observers present, you ought to be told who they are. One of the authors was once interviewed for a university post where what seemed to be as many as 23 people were sitting round a large table – three to ask questions and 20 to observe the proceedings. This is most unlikely to happen to you: the people present as observers in this case were representing all sorts of interests and at an assessment centre you will be in an entirely different situation. However, the presence of observers might bother you, so try to put them out of your mind – after all, it may be that they are only there to provide feedback on the interviewers' performance. So, concentrate your attention on the people who are asking the questions.

Dividing up the labour

Panel interviewers have the luxury of dividing up the labour and they will usually do this beforehand, that is to say, they will each agree to take responsibility for a particular area. So one might ask questions around a certain competency, another might dig into some aspect of your CV such as your previous jobs, and another might follow up matters that have arisen from the tests and inventories you have done.

Rapport

Good interviewers will immediately try to strike up a rapport with you. This is more difficult to do in a panel interview, both for them and for you. This is because it takes time for each interviewer to build up a rapport with the candidate and if they are not careful they will achieve little else in the time available. So, for their part, they have to strike a balance between establishing rapport with you and pressing ahead with asking questions aimed at obtaining the evidence on which to make judgements about you. From your point of view you need to remember that although prime responsibility rests with the panel members to establish rapport with you, building rapport is a two-way process. So, you should try to respond positively to each individual attempt at building rapport.

It may turn out that you are interviewed by just two people, in which case there is the possibility of achieving some rapport quite quickly. It usually starts with a question that is intended as an icebreaker. One of the interviewers might pick up on something spotted in your application form or CV. 'I see you like to go bungee jumping. I do too. Have you ever tried the North Face of the Eiger?' If something like this happens to you, be grateful for it, but don't go overboard in your response. For example, you might say 'I hear it can be very tricky in winter', and leave it at that.

One of the authors was once interviewing a person with a background in marketing. Her CV showed that she had been responsible for marketing a certain soft drink. When, at the start of the interview, he told her that he and his family liked that drink – in fact couldn't get enough of it – she relaxed visibly and said 'Let me send you a case. Is it the guava or the mango that does it for you?' Needless to say, the promised case never arrived, but that short interaction succeeded in breaking the ice both for her and the interviewer.

Non-verbal signs

Once the interview has started, look out for signs that the interviewers are interested and are giving you maximum attention. Non-verbal signs (sometimes called 'body language') that convey this message include nodding of the head, smiling and looking intently at you (but not staring). The signs that indicate that they are not paying attention you can probably imagine for yourself. Yawning is one of the worst, especially when they try to conceal it behind a raised hand. Yet, however much you might want to say 'am I keeping you up?' you must hold your tongue and press on with what you are saying. Hopefully you will not encounter behaviour of this kind at an assessment centre – because of their professional expertise the people who are there should know better. Anyway, at a panel interview there is a good chance that someone, through his or her body language, is giving you some encouragement. Of course the converse is that if no one is responding positively to what you are saying you are probably struggling to make an impact on them, in which case you may have to make an effort to improve matters.

Before the interview

It is to your advantage to do some preliminary research in preparation for the interview. For example, if you do not already belong to the organization, try to find out:

- what the company or organization does;
- what the company produces or what services it provides;
- the company's origins;
- where the company's operating base is located;
- the type and number of company employees;
- current initiatives and new products and services;
- who the head of the organization is;
- any recent press comment.

You should be able to obtain this kind of information from the company's or organization's Web site.

Think about what you might be asked in the interview and prepare some answers to take the sting out of the tougher questions that might otherwise surprise you:

- Why have you applied for this job?
- Why did you choose the course you did at college/university?
- Which aspects of the course did you find most enjoyable, least enjoyable, most difficult, least difficult and why?
- What are you looking for in a job?
- What are your strengths?
- What are you weaknesses?
- When you have had a deadline to meet, what have you done to ensure that you have met the deadline?
- When you have had to choose a partner or team members to work with on a project, how did you go about making the choice?

- What do you think makes a good team?
- Why would others want to have you on their team?
- What would you do if a team member was not pulling her or his weight?
- How did the members of your research group co-ordinate their efforts?
- Tell me about a time when something has not gone well for you – what did you do to overcome this? What would you do differently next time?
- How do you see this job fitting into your career path?
- What other jobs have you applied for? How are your applications progressing?
- Why do you want to leave your current job? (When answering do not to be too negative about your current employer – you could end up giving a preview of how well you complain, which would not go down too well.)
- What sort of things put you under pressure? Give me an example and tell me how you cope.
- What would your colleagues say about you?
- Tell me about a presentation you have done – how did you prepare for it? What went well? What went badly?
- What do you know about this organization?

You should also be prepared to answer questions about your health, more technical questions related to your qualifications, research or current job, plus any interests you have mentioned on your CV or application form. So, when compiling your CV or filling in an application form bear in mind that anything you say about yourself might become the subject of some searching questions in an interview.

How to 'foul up' at the interview

A recent survey by the recruitment people Office Angels pinpointed three key areas where interviewees consistently fail to impress: inappropriate dress (30 per cent); arrogance (27 per cent); and monosyllabic responses (25 per cent). Indeed, candidates even seem to be getting the simplest things wrong: almost half (48 per cent) of the employers claimed that they had had people arrive late for interviews without even offering an apology. These areas clearly matter to employers so it is worth taking some time to look at them more closely.

Arrogance

In the eye of the beholder, arrogance comprises a multitude of sins. It is anything that might attract the descriptors 'cocky', 'pushy', 'uppity', 'self-centred', 'on his or her own agenda'. Basically, what employers are criticizing is a lack of humility, an attitude that conveys a sense of knowing it all, of having nothing to learn, summed up by 'take me as I am' – in short, what is often called 'attitude'. Obviously, it is not in your best interest to project an image of this kind through your behaviour in an interview. If you know or suspect that you may come across to others as having 'attitude' then you should try to modify your behaviour accordingly. However, beware of over-compensating because then you will not be being true to yourself and that will be readily apparent to an experienced interview panel. Figure 5.1 gives some examples of answers that can be construed as arrogant.

The situation is complicated by the fact that interviewers are often partial to what they see as a bit of 'personality' or 'charisma'. Indeed they sometimes say that they are looking for

✗   I don't need to prepare. I just look at it and I know it.

✗   I get on well with other people. It is they who don't seem to get on with me.

✗   I have shown that I can lead a group of people – why should this job be any different?

✗   You don't need to be able to juggle figures. We have computers to do that.

✗   Are you really? (In answer to someone who introduces themselves with their name.)

✗   I know who I am and I like it.

Figure 5.1   Answers that can be construed as arrogant

that in preference to 'dull clones'. But if the observed behaviour is not served up quite how they like it they start to label it as 'arrogance'. So, just be aware that it is risky to go into an interview too full of confidence – there is a thin line for you to tread between presenting an 'attitude' that is admired and one that is admonished. What employers call 'arrogance' is a collection of behaviours that is best described as 'inappropriate'. This can be illustrated by the following account.

One of the interviewers at a panel interview had a heavy cold and apologized in advance to the four candidates in case he sounded husky or indistinct or both. Three of the four candidates said things like 'I'm sorry' or 'I sympathize, I've just got over one' or even 'There's a lot of it about'. The fourth candidate did nothing of the sort. When offered the apology he immediately shifted his chair back and put his hands in front of his face as if to ward off the germs. Interviews are certainly a two-way process, but on this occasion the candidate's behaviour went well beyond that. It succeeded in embarrassing the interviewer, and a riposte along the lines of 'Don't worry, I'm not infectious' had to be made. As for the interview itself, the candidate was bright and sharp and energetic but so were the others. The difference was that they didn't get 'cocky' and 'presumptuous' written against their names in the evaluation notes. So remember, it's not worth trying to show off – far better to show that you are both tactful and socially aware.

Monosyllabic responses

You must be prepared to open up – that is the point of an interview. If employers wanted 'yes' or 'no' answers they would have sent you a questionnaire and would not have invited you to attend an interview. To respond in this way is to impose self-inflicted wounds on yourself and to limit your chances of success, however well you have performed on the other assessment centre activities. So why do it?

The interview itself

Enter the room confidently. Don't sidle in as if you would prefer not to be noticed. When greeting the panel look the interviewers in the eyes and smile. If the panel chair offers her or his hand, take it and then shake hands with the other panel members.

During the interview concentrate, listen actively, be positive and enthusiastic. Make good eye contact, sit alertly and try to ident, even if you don't feel it! Behave as if it is the job opportunity of a lifetime and that you are keen to avail yourself of it. Do not fidget or lose eye contact by gazing out of the window. Ask relevant questions. Most importantly don't be afraid to sell yourself. You may need what they have to offer more than they need you!

To sum up, in order to get a good result at the panel interview, this is what you need to do:

- give your full attention;
- listen to the questions – and answer them as fully and honestly as you can;
- take each point in turn and ask for clarification if necessary;
- say if you don't know the answer;
- don't give one word answers, such as 'yes' and 'no' – try to elaborate;
- use 'I' not 'we', unless you are talking about working with others in a team.

When it is your turn to ask questions, use it as an opportunity to show what you know about the organization and to clarify any areas of uncertainty about the job.

Don't be afraid to bring a list of questions with you. Don't ask too many questions, but make sure that you find out as much as you need to know about the job or the opportunity for further training that is on offer.

Types of questions that interviewers ask

Since the primary objective of the interview is to obtain evidence from you, it follows that you should do most of the talking. Specifically, the panel should aim to have you talking approximately 70 to 80 per cent of the time. The knack lies in the type of questions they ask.

Open questions

Open questions enable you to provide facts and information, describe events, express feelings or opinions, etc. In short, they get you talking. For example 'Tell me about the duties in your present job', or 'How did you deal with an irate member of the public?'

To each of these open questions you will find it very difficult (unless you are wedded to the monosyllabic response) to avoid being drawn into a stream of talk that is more or less informative according to how well you do it. Fortunately, one of the saving graces of questions of this kind is that the topics on which they are based are fairly predictable, in which case you should be well prepared for them. That should enable you to seize the initiative by imposing a structure on your answer that is to your advantage. For example, in response to the first question given above you might begin by saying 'According to my current job description I have four main areas of responsibility... but in reality I find most of my time is taken up with...'

Closed questions

The closed question is different. To these questions you can answer 'yes' or 'no' and in both cases the answer would be a sufficient reply. Two examples are 'Did you enjoy your last job?' and 'Did you get on well with your supervisor?'

Closed questions are useful for checking your understanding of answers, or checking specific facts, but are not good for getting you to open up and talk. If you find interviewers overusing the closed question you can always – if you think it will help you – expand on your answer without being explicitly bidden to do so. In such a situation, it is a good idea to proceed tentatively, for example by saying 'I would like to develop that point further if I may' or by asking 'Before I answer the question directly would it be helpful if I said something first about the situation in which I was working?'

Multiple-headed questions

These occur when two or more questions are asked in one go. For example, 'Why have you applied for this job, where do you see yourself in five years' time, and why do you want to leave your present job?' On these occasions, the temptation is to focus on the question you would prefer to answer and to ignore those that you consider to be more awkward (or revealing of your weaknesses). It will not have escaped your notice that politicians are very adept at doing this! Of course it is possible to respond in such a way as to address all of questions. For example, in response to the questions asked above you might begin by saying 'The reasons why I am considering leaving my present job are related to the factors that led to my applying for this post, and in turn that is related to the position I would like to be in in five years' time.' Having set up your response in that way you can then proceed to identify those aspects of the job being offered, including the personal development and career progression opportunities promised in the details that have been provided.

Leading questions

This is where the answer to the question is given away in the question itself. This usually occurs where the interviewer prefaces the question with some information either from the job description or the person specification. For example: 'In this job you have to lick a lot of stamps – how do you feel about licking stamps?' or 'We are looking for somebody who can work to deadlines – how well do you work to deadlines?' If you are lucky enough to get questions like these, make the most of them but stop this side of being glib. The following would be over the top: 'Licking stamps – I love it. I can never get enough of it. I would count it a poor day if I did not lick some stamps.' 'Deadlines – they're a doddle. I eat deadlines. If I didn't have deadlines, I couldn't get out of bed in the morning.' And so on.

Hypothetical questions

This is where the interviewer describes a situation to you and asks you what you would do in the circumstances. They really ought to be asking you how you handled similar situations in the past rather than trying to see how you might handle a situation in the future. So, rather than asking 'How would you deal with an irate customer if you were faced with one?' they should ask: 'Can you give me an example of when you had to deal with an irate member of the public?' However, if you are asked a hypothetical question you will know what to say – 'I would remain calm, write down the details and promise to contact a senior colleague immediately', or some such thing.

Multiple-choice questions

This is the oral equivalent of a multiple-choice item in a written test. It is where the interviewer asks a question and provides the candidate with a number of answers to select from. For example: 'How did you find out about this job? Was it through the Job Centre, your careers teacher, an advertisement, a friend who already works for the company, or what?' Here the inter-viewer is doing all the work for you – so let him (or her). Quite often the first part of the question (in this case, 'How did you find out about this job?') is good enough on its own. It is essen-tial, therefore, to listen carefully to what the questioner is saying.

Turning a weakness into a strength

Watch out for this. People have gone on record saying this is how you score with interviewers, but don't be too sure. You might think you are being very clever, but competent inter-viewers will quickly see through you. 'What are your weak-nesses?', you are asked, and you reply along the lines, 'I ask too much of myself and of others so when they fail to deliver I get disappointed. I am afraid that my standards are just too high for some people'. You may think you have finessed the question beautifully, but the interviewers are all too likely to have noted 'unwilling to reveal and discuss weaknesses'.

Systematic interviewing around competencies

We mentioned that you should expect in an assessment centre to be interviewed systematically around competencies, or such-like. An example of a question set for the competency 'achievement drive' would be: 'In the preparation form, you described a situation where you achieved something difficult. Tell me a little about this...'

● Why did you pursue this particular objective?
● What setbacks did you encounter? How did you work through them?

● Was anyone else involved? How did you motivate them to work with you?
● What was the outcome?

The interviewers might repeat these questions for the second example if more evidence is required. They may also throw in additional questions, like: 'Could you describe a time when you have tried to accomplish something, but failed?'

● How did the situation arise?
● What did you learn?
● How have you put this into practice?

'Describe a time when you have accomplished a task through effective utilization of others.'

● Who else was involved?
● What was your approach?
● What difficulties did you face? How did you deal with them?
● How did it all turn out?

What the interviewer is doing here is what is known as 'going down the funnel'. In other words, the interviewer is probing away at you and in the course of this is taking you down an imaginary funnel, the idea being to reach the bottom of what you have to say.

This method is designed to provide specific behavioural evidence of what you have done in the past. By asking about real events, the skilled interviewer should be able to identify behavioural patterns as well as whether you are simply 'talking a good game'. Your answers are later analysed and marked against the behavioural indicators relating to that competency.

The interview may not obviously be driven by a competency framework. The panel may decide to work through your CV in a chronological way. If that happens, you can expect them to (among other things) explore your experience, your reasons for job changes or other significant decisions, and your aspirations. Although the interview is structured by time, it is still important that the panel has a clear set of criteria (such as competencies) against which to evaluate the information gained. If not, this can quickly become an unstructured interview – 'Oh, I see you hunted giant mallard in Tadzhikistan (or went over the Victoria Falls in a washing-up bowl); I bet that was exciting.' This is the kind of interview that is often favoured by head-hunters.

Killer questions

Beware of surprise questions such as 'Why should I employ you rather than another candidate?' and so-called 'killer questions'. In an ideal world you should not have to face them, but it looks as if they have become standard practice. In a recent survey by Office Angels of over 500 UK employers, 75 per cent of employers admitted that they ask a 'killer question'.

According to employers, these questions are not designed to deliberately catch people out, but rather to encourage those in the 'hot seat' to think on their feet. With over two thirds (68 per cent) of interviewers claiming candidates could be better prepared and show greater enthusiasm, answering these questions confidently, they say, could mean the difference between 'make or break'.

Here are some examples of 'killer questions' asked by employers:

● Tell us a joke.

- What was the question you didn't want us to ask you?
- Would you ever lie in the interests of your job?
- Give us three things to remember you by.
- Name the members of the Cabinet.

You don't really want to get involved with questions like these. But if you want the job badly enough you might have to answer them. Of course, you might decide there and then that you do not want to work for an organization that permits or even encourages such questions to be asked. That is your prerogative and you would be entitled to register your disapproval and, if really riled, leave (not a good idea because the panel members might admire your stand and offer you the job anyway).

In our estimation you are much less likely to encounter 'killer questions' in an assessment centre. If the interviewers have organized themselves properly (which you can't necessarily assume) they should be asking you questions derived systematically from an interview schedule that is based around competencies with names like 'planning and organizing', 'results focus', and 'judgement'.

Interview checklist – dos and don'ts

- Do plenty of research about the organization before your interview.
- Make a note of your interviewers' names and positions – potentially one of them could be your new boss.
- Arrive ahead of time.
- Dress smartly and remember to smile – this instantly creates a good impression.

- Be yourself within reason (but if 'yourself' is full of 'attitude' don't bother).
- Listen carefully to the questions and answer them as honestly as possible.
- Make good eye contact with your interviewers.
- Be confident and alert.
- Make sure you find out as much as you need to about what is on offer with regard to the job or developmental opportunity for which you have applied.
- Don't ask too many questions, but ask some questions.
- Don't use 'yes' and 'no' as answers – try to elaborate.
- Don't be afraid to prepare a list of questions in advance of your interview.
- Don't gabble – speak slowly and clearly.

Chapter 6

How to succeed on in-tray, case study and role play exercises

The aim of this chapter is to acquaint you with the different types of in-tray, case study, and role play exercises that you might encounter at an assessment centre and to help you prepare for them.

In-tray exercises

The basic idea is that you are given a set of material typical of that which might be found in a manager's in-tray at work. You then have a certain amount of time to deal with each item in that in-tray. Assessment is usually by means of a detailed scoring procedure but can be augmented in some cases by a debriefing interview.

In-tray exercises are useful for purposes of personnel selection because they:

- are quite realistic and representative of the tasks people encounter in their work roles;
- produce a sample of behaviour over a range of tasks;
- provide evidence about a variety of competencies;
- can be linked to other activities in an assessment-centre programme such as role-play exercises, telephone conversations and group discussion.

It is useful to know that the following issues feature in in-tray exercises used for selection purposes: health and safety; maintaining output; the delivery of services to clients; labour relations in the workplace; relations with the public; handling customers and their complaints; responding to queries or instructions from senior management, and environmental impact.

In-tray exercises are not as popular perhaps as they once were and you may not be given one. If they are waning in popularity it is probably because there is a growing acceptance that the majority of tasks they are simulating are now done electronically without the need to shuffle pieces of paper. All that means, however, is that in future electronic in-tray exercises can be expected to feature in the personnel selection procedures used at assessment centres. In fact, examples are already known to be in use.

It is difficult for you to practise for this particular assessment centre exercise unless someone is prepared to assemble a typical set of in-tray materials for you and then discuss with you how you might deal with them in a workplace context. There are, however, two main things of which you need to be aware. First, you will have to work within strict time limits, during which you will have to:

- read each item (there can be as many as 20);

- make a decision about what action you would recommend in each case;
- keep a record of all your decisions and the reasoning behind them.

Second, the contents of the in-tray are interconnected – an action recommended for one item may well have repercussions on others.

The following example has been chosen to illustrate these points and if you work your way through it, you will get the general idea.

Example of an in-tray scenario

You are an employee of Kidsplace, producer and distributor of playthings for children. Coinciding with the appointment last year of a new managing director, the company has diversified into collectable cards and figures hoping – let's be frank – to climb on the bandwagon that is (or maybe was) Pokémon. For the past six months sets of cards and figures have been tested in three regions of the UK.

While Pokémon was going strong the outlook for these products was good but the market is volatile and the MD will soon have to take a decision as to whether to go deeper into this market, or look elsewhere.

Presently, you are a member of a small team within sales and marketing. You share a secretary and an assistant with the others. Most of your work is to do with supporting existing brands but from time to time you are asked to help evaluate new brand ideas. You get involved more than most in this activity. The MD will also be relying on you for help with market data and trends as she weighs up her investment decision.

It is 9.00 am on Monday, 28 July and you have just returned from two weeks' leave to find a quite full in-tray. In the forefront of your mind is a meeting that you are due to have in two hours' time with the rest of the team including your immediate manager. A few items in your in-tray are bound to come up at that meeting but you don't know which ones. So you need to be prepared.

Your task is:

- To go through your in-tray prioritizing the items in the order you intend to deal with them. A sheet is provided for you to write down the order, starting at the top and working down (the items are numbered). You should also specify the type of action you intend to take and what the justification for that action is.
- Once you have established an order, start to work your way through the items in the time available (90 minutes).
- Do not make the mistake of putting off everything, or nearly everything. You should make an effort to work through most of the items. If you have to defer making a telephone call, say why, and until when.

Provided for your use are memo blanks and telephone message blanks. If you want to telephone someone, write out what you would want to say on the message blank.

Contents of the in-tray

That, then, is how an in-tray is set up. There will typically be 20 or so items to work through. All will be designed to make demands on your time and judgement. It is unlikely that you can deal with everything so it is up to you to optimize your output. The exact items may vary but you can expect to find in your tray some or all of the following:

- A letter from a concerned-parents' group bemoaning the commercial exploitation of young children (they really mean the parents). Pokémon, they say, already costs far too much. Your job will be to draft a reply for someone higher up to sign (or maybe ask someone else to do it).

- Some items that, on the face of it, look trivial but actually require some thought and attention – quick judgement calls really – like whether to attend the Gdansk Toy Fair where competitors are exhibiting next week, or a complaint from another department about the shared secretary (is this your business or the team's and how do you deal with it?).

- One or two items of a social nature, which may contain the seeds of conflict with more obviously work-related activities.

- An item with a personal tinge where, again, there may be a stretch on your time if you are to keep all or most of the balls in the air.

- An enquiry from the sales director as to whether the company should be pushing cards or figures and on what evidence.

- An item suggesting that some internal strife is brewing. You (say you are Sam) are expecting help from a colleague (suppose it is Viv) in compiling data for the MD, but is that help going to be forthcoming? A somewhat airy note from Viv suggests not and leaves you uneasy and frankly a bit put out.

- A request from the MD for a meeting next Monday to find out how the report is shaping up. (What report? Help!)

- Bits of disparate data from the publicity and cuttings people that have to be processed and massaged into that report.

And so it goes. Nor may that be all. Those fiendishly cunning assessment centre designers may ordain that at some time during the in-tray exercise you will be presented with new items, maybe entirely new or, more likely, pertaining to items already in the in-tray that you might already have processed. What must you do then? Well, you press on and, in so doing, try to show the assessors that you are capable of dealing with a multiplicity of things simultaneously – and coping with unexpected contingencies should they arise.

Last word on the in-tray

In practice, there would be a key for evaluating the quality of your decisions. You would be assessed in terms of whether your views on what should be considered high, medium or low priority coincide with those of expert assessors. Even so, whose priority? That is where you need a sense of reality and expediency. Remember, when doing in-tray exercises, always try to think strategically by seeking to link up as many items as you can – to kill two (or more) birds with one stone.

Case study exercises

A case study is a realistic and relevant business problem. Candidates typically are asked to analyse the problem, interpret data, consider alternatives, and produce a written report describing their solutions or recommendations.

Exercises based on case studies are useful because they:

● provide a reasonably direct measure of relevant skills;
● are convenient to administer – can be done in groups;
● are easy to interpret – detailed performance indicators can be provided;
● are relatively easy to construct and customize.

The competencies that the case study exercise is intended to evaluate will have been given names like 'analytical thinking', 'perspective and judgement', 'planning and organizing', and 'communication'. Thus, the assessors will judge your performance using a set of indicators organized around headings such as these. If you are at all unsure about how you measure up against these competencies we suggest that you revisit the self-audit given in Appendix 1. In so doing you would be advised to pay particular attention to the following categories: oral and written communication skills; planning and prioritizing work; making decisions, and problem solving.

Example of a case study

You can imagine how easily a case study could be developed out of the Kidsplace scenario. What would happen is that you (as Sam) would be furnished with the statistics already in the in-tray plus a whole lot of other information, some of which has been filtered through Viv (there is friction between you and Viv, but that is the subject of the role-play exercise discussed below). Your task would then be to prepare a strategic report for the MD.

Role plays

These are one-to-one exercises where the candidate conducts an interview or meeting with a role player who has been given a thorough briefing. The role play is observed by an assessor or assessors (although it could be videotaped). The assessor may question the candidate afterwards to find out more about the strategy, direction and outcome of the interview/meeting.

Role play exercises of this kind have several advantages when it comes to personnel selection, in particular they:

● allow observation of 'people skills';
● are realistic, especially for managerial tasks;
● can be tailored to suit a range of tasks and situations.

The disadvantage is that candidates may feel that they have been put in a false situation and that they lack the background knowledge from which to determine tactics. Role play exercises are also said to be unpopular with candidates who have been heard to complain that if they had wanted to be actors they would have done so – a view with which the assessors will have little or no sympathy.

Use of actors

An interesting development is the use of professional role players, usually actors, to play roles opposite the candidate. It has been our experience that candidates are invariably bowled over by what these actors bring to the assessment situation and this, in itself, contributes greatly to validating the assessment for candidates.

An example

Again, we return to the Kidsplace company. The best assessment centre designers always try to have a theme and threads running right through the programme. This helps you because it means that you have to immerse yourself in just one workplace context rather than several.

As already mentioned, there is friction, maybe even bad blood, between Sam and Viv. You get a sense of it from the in-tray items, especially the airy note from Viv. Plainly, you, as Sam, are expecting a sizeable input from Viv to your report for the MD but it does not look as if you are going to get it. The subject of the role play is therefore a 'clear the air' meeting – let us not call it a confrontation – with Viv. It will be a one-on-one meeting. You will play Sam and an actor will play Viv.

The actor's briefing

The actor will be closely briefed as to how to respond to you. Here is an example of the kind of briefing that actors are given.

One-to-one role play exercises demand a high level of skill and preparation on the part of the role player if they are to be effective. The role player is there to enable the participant to demonstrate his or her strengths in face-to-face situations. Thus the role player needs to be sufficiently restrained to present a challenge to the participant yet not be so obstructive that the participant has no chance to resolve the issues. Further-more, the role must be played consistently with different partic-ipants, to ensure fairness and permit valid comparisons to be made.

Specifically, these are the kind of guidelines actors get to encourage them to maintain an objective approach:

- It is important that you give a consistent performance throughout – do not vary the role you are playing (aggres-sive to one participant, mild to another).
- It is a reactive role. The initiative rests with the participant and you should react naturally to the comments made. If they annoy you, be annoyed but do not go over the top; if they make you feel at ease then respond accordingly.
- Try to let the participant lead, except when directed to the contrary by the brief.

- If the participant is struggling then assist by giving appropriate information to keep the discussion moving.
- If the discussion ends early then let it end.
- Make sure you can see the time. Keep track of the time and bring the discussion to a close at the end of the period allowed.
- Allow participants to develop arguments. (Give the participant thinking time; do not interrupt too frequently.)
- Certain ploys can be useful to stretch a participant, for example 'I'm surprised to hear you say that. My previous team leaders never raised that as an issue.'
- Stay within the intentions/feelings of the brief. If the answer is not in the brief, then make up the answer from your experience but do not stray into new issues. Maintain the focus detailed in the brief.

So you can see that essentially the actor's job is to be reactive to whatever you say. The actor will be given a series of 'buttons' that she or he can press depending on what you say and how the meeting goes. If you lose your temper with Viv the actor will be told what to do (trade blows or stay cool according to how you play it). Viv will, of course, have a defence and you might not know everything about this. It might especially centre around other demands on his or her time. She or he could throw facts at you that might be a surprise and you will have to respond constructively to this. This is not a black-and-white scenario where you are wronged and Viv is the perpetrator – but you can play it like that if you choose and see how far you get.

In the end, you and Viv have to get on, and you have to produce a report for the MD. The last thing you want to do is to go to her crying foul (although you might have already done so in your in-tray exercise). So you have to make up and work out how to do the best you can in the time available.

What to do in role plays

You will usually be given something like 30 minutes to prepare. In this kind of one-on-one with undercurrents of friction or resentment (there are others although this is often the kind you will get), try to:

● get in role, don't be half in and half out;
● take the other role player(s) seriously;
● be civil, not angry from the word go;
● have a plan and stick to it (more or less);
● plan to extract some agreement (concessions?) from the other person;
● work out how you are going to close the meeting;
● have a clear idea of next steps and write them down;
● be firm, never petulant.

Chapter 7

After an assessment centre: how to achieve future success

The aim of this concluding chapter is to provide you with guidance on:

- obtaining feedback on how you performed at an assessment centre;
- evaluating your experience;
- using the outcomes of self-review as the basis for the purposes of personal development;
- achieving future success.

Seeking feedback from others

As a participant at an assessment centre it may well be that you are not given a decision about whether or not you have been selected before you leave – that will come later in the form of a telephone call or a letter. However, you should expect to be given some form of feedback on how well you performed. Indeed, a short debriefing session may well have been structured into the programme (see Figure 1.2) for precisely this purpose.

If you find that the assessors do not intend to offer you feedback before you depart, you should be prepared to take the initiative and ask for it. Their willingness to respond positively will no doubt be related to a number of factors, including the manner in which you make your request and how busy the person is with other commitments at the time. With regard to the former, it would not go amiss to begin by offering your thanks for the experiences afforded to you at the assessment centre prior to making your request for some feedback on your performance. This may well be seized on as an opportunity to open up a dialogue with you, which would be beneficial to both sides – as professionals the assessors should be just as keen as you are to receive some evaluative feedback on the event. If, however, the time and circumstances are not favourable you would be well advised to indicate that you appreciate their situation and ask if it would be possible for you to telephone at a mutually convenient time.

If you have already been told that you have not been selected, you should try to overcome your immediate sense of disappointment. You will be better served by adopting a positive frame of mind in which you think of this as the starting point for your preparation for the next assessment centre rather than dwell on your apparent 'failure' at the last one. After all, at an assessment centre, success or lack of it is always relative – you might have performed as well as you thought and to the best of your ability, but you might still have lost out to another candidate for reasons best known to the assessors.

Feedback process

It is important to remember with feedback that it takes two sides to make it effective – the giving and the receiving. If the assessor is skilled at giving feedback the chances are that he or she will give you a clear indication of:

● how well you performed overall;
● how well you coped with the individual assessment exercises;
● what you need to work on in order to improve your performance;
● what your developmental priorities should be if you are to succeed at your next assessment centre.

If the assessors do not volunteer useful feedback of this kind, it is up to you to use your oral communication and interpersonal skills to extract it from them.

So much for the 'giving', what about the 'receiving'? In this respect you be well advised to:

● listen carefully to the feedback even if you find it uncomfortable;
● try not be too defensive by immediately rejecting what has been said or arguing with the person providing the feedback;
● make a mental note of points of disagreement or questions you wish to ask so that you can check them out later;
● make sure that you understand the feedback before you respond to it – a useful and effective way of doing this is to paraphrase or repeat what the person has said in order to check that you have understood;
● ask questions to clarify what has been said if you do not understand the feedback you have been given;

- ask for feedback on specific aspects of your performance that you would find useful;
- reflect on the feedback you have been given and on the basis of your evaluation decide how best you can use it.

Above all, try to avoid 'selective hearing syndrome' as illustrated in the following conversation:

First person: 'You are the most intelligent, humorous, compassionate, witty and considerate person I have EVER met. I prefer your company to that of anyone else even though you are a bit moody sometimes.'

Second person: 'What do you mean by a bit moody sometimes?'

Finally, remember to thank the person who has gone to the trouble of providing you with feedback – it does no harm to show your appreciation for what he or she has done.

Self-review – evaluating your assessment-centre experience

Your aim should now be to reflect on your assessment centre experience in the light of the feedback you have been given, with a view to devising an action plan for your personal development. The purpose of that plan should be to increase your chances of success at your next assessment centre. In devising that plan you would be well advised to:

- reflect systematically on your experiences and the feedback you received;

- record the key points to emerge from that reflection;
- use the outcomes as the basis for identifying the action you need to take in order to improve your future performance at an assessment centre.

Developing a self-improvement action plan

The use of a framework like the one given in Figure 7.1 could help you with this self-review process. In particular, it should help you to identify a set of action points that have been generated through a process of structured reflection. You will, of course, need to turn those action points into a coherent action plan in which you set yourself some targets. With regard to those targets our advice would be to make them **SMART**:

S = specific;
M = manageable;
A = appropriate and achievable;
R = relevant, realistic and recorded;
T = time limited.

In other words, you need to proceed as systematically in devising an action plan for your own self-improvement as you were in reflecting on your experiences. If you are capable of doing that and translating that plan into effective action you will increase your chances of success at your next assessment centre. You will also have learned some important lessons about managing your own continuous development and becoming a lifelong learner – attributes that are increasingly valued by employers.

Assessment centre experiences	Evaluation feedback	Action to be taken
Planning and preparation	Assessor said I was caught out too often (eg in the interview) by lack of background knowledge about the organization and details of work involved.	Make sure that I have studied details of the organization (eg Web page) and that I am familiar with the job specification.
Ability tests	Assessor said that I lost marks by failing to complete both tests; I felt I could have answered the questions correctly had I not run out of time.	
Personality inventory		
Group discussion exercise		
Presentation		
Case study: in-tray exercise		
Interview		

Figure 7.1 Assessment centre self-review framework

Appendix 1: auditing your skills

'Success in the knowledge economy comes to those who know themselves – their strengths, their values, and how best to perform.' (Drucker, P (1999) Managing yourself, *Harvard Business Review*, March–April, pp 65–74.)

Look at each of the statements below and try to decide how competent you are at each of the skills. Record your decision by placing a tick in the appropriate box in the table, where:

1 = I am very good at this
2 = I can do this most of the time, but with some difficulty
3 = I need to work on this in order to improve

1 Oral communication skills

		1	2	3
a	I know when to listen and when to speak			
b	I speak in a clear, concise and confident manner			
c	I know how to pitch what I am saying to suit the audience			
d	I can deal effectively with questions			
e	I can elicit information through effective questioning			
f	I know when to use the telephone and when to write			
g	I can deal with difficult people			
h	I can identify and take account of any 'hidden agendas'			

2 Written communication skills

		1	2	3
a	My writing is clear, concise and confident			
b	I pitch the message to suit the audience			
c	I know when to write and when to speak			
d	When I make written recommendations they are clearly expressed and easily understood			
e	I know how to gauge the length and complexity of documents I write			
f	I know when to terminate correspondence			

3 Numeracy

		1	2	3
a	I can prepare estimates with reasonable accuracy			
b	I know when to estimate and when to calculate exactly			
c	I can recognize dubious statistical arguments or presentations			
d	I can convert data from one format to another			
e	I can use quantitative evidence as necessary			
f	I check solutions for plausibility			
g	I understand the limitations of statistical data			

4 Information and communication technology (ICT)

		1	2	3
a	I can process information using a variety of software packages			
b	I can combine information from different sources including text, images, graphs and charts			
c	I can create automated routines to aid the efficient processing of information			
d	I can make efficient use of e-mail, including the sending of attachments			
e	I can present information effectively on the Web			
f	I can improve presentations through the use of packages such as Powerpoint			
g	I can assess information from a variety of sources, including database, CD-ROMs and the Internet			
h	I can store information using directories and folders and can retrieve it as and when required			
i	I can evaluate the effectiveness of the procedures I use and introduce modifications to improve my performance			

5 Planning and prioritizing work

		1	2	3
a	I prepare and plan well in advance			
b	I have contingency plans against possible setbacks			
c	I meet deadlines and get the job done			
d	I keep work moving			
e	When delegating I use the time of others effectively			
f	I can bring projects in on time			
g	I am capable of doing several things simultaneously (eg working, studying, outside interests)			

6 Adapting to and managing change

		1	2	3
a	I am positive when asked 'What would you do if…?'			
b	I can adapt to change			
c	I can produce ideas and solutions to problems created by change			
d	I can see when changes need to be made and can take appropriate action			
e	I can think on my feet without panicking			

7 Making decisions

		1	2	3
a	I take personal responsibility for the consequences of my own actions and decisions			
b	I take decisions at the appropriate time			
c	I am aware that new information may cause judgements to be modified			
d	I do not back off making decisions in situations of ambiguity and uncertainty			
e	I seek different kinds of information so that I can make better judgements			
f	I point out the consequences of taking alternative decisions			
g	I will reconsider a decision if a case is made for doing so			
h	I refer decisions upwards when it is appropriate to do so			

8 Getting on with people

		1	2	3
a	I challenge alternative viewpoints calmly and rationally			
b	I am able to work co-operatively with others from various functions and backgrounds			
c	I am willing to give way in the interests of team goals and harmony			
d	I am aware of the impact I can have on others			
e	I recognize the need to build constructive relationships with people			
f	I actively encourage two-way communication, avoiding 'put downs' and destructive criticism			
g	I can make other people feel valued			

9 Influencing/negotiating

		1	2	3
a	I convey personal commitment and belief when presenting my own viewpoint			
b	I put together reasoned, convincing arguments to support my viewpoints			
c	I anticipate possible objections and counter-arguments			
d	I assemble arguments to appeal to others' interests and concerns			

10 Flexibility/creativity

		1	2	3
a	I am able to combine different viewpoints and perspectives to produce original ideas			
b	I am able to find new and different ways to put across ideas			
c	I keep an open mind until sufficient information is available			
d	I am prepared to act as devil's advocate in order to clarify an issue			
e	I adjust my viewpoint as new evidence becomes available			

11 Problem solving

		1	2	3
a	I am aware that problems exist with no immediate solutions			
b	I can select and use appropriate methods for exploring a problem and analysing its main features			
c	I can establish the criteria that have to be met in order to show that the problem has been solved successfully			
d	I am capable of generating different options for tackling a problem			
e	I can analyse options and devise an action plan based on the option that has the most realistic chance of success			
f	I can implement my action plan, making effective use of feedback and support from others in the process			
g	I can review progress towards solving a problem and revise the approach as necessary			
h	I can check whether the criteria have been met for the successful solution of a problem			
i	I can review my approach to solving a problem, including whether alternative methods/options might have been more effective			

12 Improving your own learning and performance

		1	2	3
a	I routinely collect and record evidence that shows that I am learning from experience			
b	I am capable of identifying my own strengths and weaknesses (like filling in this audit)			
c	I can set myself personal development goals that seek to build on my strengths and address my weaknesses			
d	I am capable of devising an action plan for the achievement of those goals			
e	I deal well with setbacks			
f	I accept feedback without defensiveness			
g	I am capable of responding positively to the constructive criticism of others			
h	I can build on positive feedback			
i	I am capable of reflecting on my experiences and using the outcomes to plan future actions			